T0208188

ARE
YOU
LEADING?

ARE
YOU
LEADING?

A REFERENCE GUIDE FOR LEADERS

RAY MARTINEZ

Library of Congress Control Number: 2023912106
ISBN: Hardcover   979-8-3694-0237-5
                          Softcover   979-8-3694-0236-8
                          eBook   979-8-3694-0238-2

Contact Info:

Ray Martinez, 970-690-3686
WWW.raymartinez.com
Mailing address: 4121 Stoneridge Ct, Fort Collins, CO. 80525

Ray MARTINEZ, Former Mayor/Councilman
Fort Collins, Colorado
Raymartinez31@gmail.com
970.690.3686

Print information available on the last page.

Rev. date: 06/29/2023

To order additional copies of this book, contact:
Xlibris
844-714-8691
www.Xlibris.com
Orders@Xlibris.com
853086

CONTENTS

FOREWORD

US Congressman Bob Schaffer, headmaster at Liberty Commons High School, Fort Collins, Colorado, said the following:

> Multiple titles of authority have been applied to Ray Martinez—soldier, police officer, businessman, chairman, member of council, mayor, and more. However, he is powerful proof that authentic leadership is cultivated independently of ranks, badges, and titles. This is the essence of

Ray's lesson, legacy, and public profile in edifying leadership. Standing, in contrast, is the abundant supply of people who, having somehow obtained status, lack actual leadership stature. They are the essence of toxic leadership. This is a crucial distinction Ray Martinez underscores with credibility and aplomb for he is a superb example of one whose lifetime of service is a genuine demonstration of true stature in real leadership.

Bob Schaffer is a former member of the United States House of Representatives from the State of Colorado in the 105th Congress and the two succeeding Congresses (January 3, 1997–January 3, 2003). Schaffer was cochairman of the Congressional Ukrainian Caucus, and an outspoken leader in promoting American interests and human rights in Eastern Europe.[1]

Schaffer is currently the headmaster of Liberty Common High School in Fort Collins, Colorado. Under Schaffer's leadership, two classes have broken the state's all-time record composite ACT and SAT scores, respectively.[2][3]
https://en.wikipedia.org/wiki/Bob_Schaffer. Retrieved 2023-05-23.

1. "Congressman Schaffer Commends Ukraine for 9/11 Support." www.brama.com. Retrieved September 14, 2018.
2. "Fort Collins charter school breaks state ACT record." Coloradoan.com. August 14, 2014. Retrieved December 30, 2016.
3. "Fort Collins charter school breaks Colorado's SAT record." *Coloradoan*. Retrieved September 14, 2018.

PREFACE

Leadership is a complex and multifaceted concept that requires a variety of skills and qualities to be effective. The ability to think independently and critically, to solve problems, and to take responsibility and accountability for one's actions are all essential components of effective leadership. However, these skills alone do not make a great leader.

A great leader is also relational, an encourager, intentional, and thoughtful. They lead by doing the right thing, exemplifying leadership qualities that inspire others to follow their lead. They are passionate about what they do and have lived experiences that inform their leadership style. They understand that the credit for success belongs to the team, not just themselves.

A great leader also knows what they stand for and is able to complement and reward their team for their contributions. They lead from within, cultivating a sense of purpose and direction for themselves and their team.

You will find that many of the styles, methods, and techniques of leading may overlap each other in the different chapters. The point is that all the categories really do overlap and intertwine with each other to coalesce your style of leadership. What's important is that you develop yourself and not mimic others. Obviously, you will have many takeaways from others, but your style will propagate from your character and rearing.

This book is a comprehensive guide to leadership with a noncomplex reading format that covers all these essential qualities and skills. It is a must-read for anyone looking to improve their leadership abilities and become a more effective leader. I think you will realize that we know most of these concepts, but we need a swift kick to remind us of them and more importantly, do it.

You can listen to my podcast, *Conversations with Ray Martinez*, on Spotify, Anchor, and many other podcast carriers, along with over two hundred podcasts where you can hear my conversations. Each chapter of this book has a podcast for your listening if you are on the road or just resting your eyes.

"Successful leaders possess the unique capability of inspiring diverse teams to outperform their competitors and they seemingly accomplish this by enthusiastically exhibiting the genuine and authentic interest to learn from others," said Gerry Agnes, President and CEO of Elevations Credit Union.

"Great leaders are almost always great simplifiers who can cut through argument, debate, and doubt to offer a solution everybody can understand," said Gen. Colin Powell, former US Secretary of State.

ACKNOWLEDGMENTS

My deepest gratitude to the people who have taught me leadership throughout my life. Their unwavering guidance and support were instrumental in shaping who I am today.

To my parents, thank you for instilling in me the values of hard work, perseverance, and compassion for others. Your love and encouragement are my anchors, and I'm grateful for the sacrifices you made for me.

To my mentors, thank you for sharing your wisdom and experience. Your mentorship has helped me navigate the challenges of life and grow as a leader. Your faith in me has given me the confidence to pursue my dreams and make a positive impact on the world.

To my friends and colleagues, thank you for being there for me through thick and thin. Your support and encouragement have helped me overcome obstacles and achieve my goals.

I am especially grateful to Dr. Gil Carbajal, who once told me, "God gives us oranges, but it's up to us to peel them back." Your words have stayed with me, reminding me that we have the power to change our perspective and transform our lives. And to Coach Hal Kinard who told me in junior high school, "You can, and you will." Coach Kinard was the person who challenged me to run for mayor of Fort Collins, saying, "You can do it, and you will win."

I'm still learning and growing as a leader, and I'm grateful for the opportunities that have allowed me to do so. I hope to pay it forward by helping others who are growing in leadership. People don't grow old, but when people stop growing, they become old.

I would also like to thank the following people:

- Becky Cisneros, a retired teacher
- Reid Pope, former principal of Poudre High School
- William Lopez, former council member, county commissioner, and teacher at Poudre High School
- Chuck Hagemeister, a former counselor at Poudre High School and former Fort Collins police sergeant
- Darin Atteberry, former city manager of Fort Collins
- Ralph Smith, former Fort Collins police chief who hired me
- Stu VanMeveren, former district attorney for the Eighth Judicial District, Colorado
- Elizabeth Dunham, former Poudre High School teacher
- Dennis Baker, PhD, a retired principal from Fort Collins High School
- Sarah Kane, executive assistant for the city of Fort Collins
- Janay Carlson, executive assistant for Elevations Credit Union
- Dick Okimoto, Sixth-Degree black belt Judo teacher
- Bob Schaffer, former US congressman

Thank you all for your unwavering support, and may God bless you all abundantly.

PROLOGUE

I had the privilege of interviewing retired Rear Admiral (RADM) Peter Brown, US Coast Guard (USCG), about his perspective on leadership with experience. His career is filled with fascinating experiences and proficiency, ranging from commanding to influential sway. His wealth of knowledge can be applied to various leadership settings, whether in the business world or in military service. He sets the tone for leadership from the top down and can inspire leaders who aspire to lead with wisdom, compassion, and strategic thinking. His interview covers almost all the chapter titles of this book.

Rear Admiral Brown recently concluded a distinguished thirty-six-year military career, serving as the deputy assistant to the president for National Security Affairs and the Homeland Security and Counterterrorism advisor. Additionally, he was the US president's senior representative for Puerto Rico's disaster recovery. He was chosen for these challenging roles due to his extensive experience in leading the Coast Guard and interagency teams in various border security, counterdrug, emergency response, and international cooperation missions.

As an expert advisor, he provided invaluable counsel on diverse homeland security threats, events, and issues to the US president, vice president, and national security advisor. During his tenure, he led five directorates of the National Security Council, including border and transportation security, counterterrorism (including counterdrug and transnational organized crime), cybersecurity, chemical/biological threats and WMD, and emergency response and resilience.

RADM Brown is always quick to give credit where it is due. Here is the first quote he made to me, "The essence of leadership is setting the conditions for others' success." I heard this from USCG Rear Admiral Norm Saunders when he was Seventh District commander (1997–99) and I was a mid-grade officer at a subordinate unit. Twenty years later, I had the honor and privilege of commanding the Seventh District, aided by the benefit of learning from leaders like Norm Saunders and others.

RADM Brown commanded a large area. The Seventh Coast Guard District encompasses South Carolina, Georgia, the Florida Peninsula, Puerto Rico, and the US Virgin Islands and is responsible for all Coast Guard operations and personnel in that region. The Seventh District commander, staff, and units also coordinate and conduct operations with thirty-four neighboring countries and territories in the Caribbean, making it the busiest operational region in the service.

The geography of the Seventh District—1.8 million square miles encompassing the entire Caribbean Sea—makes it vulnerable to tropical storms and hurricanes. Over Labor Day weekend in 2017, rapidly strengthening Hurricane Irma tracked steadily westward toward the Caribbean, threatening Puerto Rico, the USVI, neighboring Caribbean Islands, and later, Florida. Convening his senior staff officers in person, and ten senior field unit commanding officers via conference call, RADM Brown assessed his team's readiness for the approaching hurricane and issued his strategic guidance to his crew.

1. Preparation phase:
   - Initiate and maintain communications with industry, interagency, state, local, and international partners.
   - Initiate early evacuation of dependents (family members) from forecast areas of storm impacts.
   - Harden or reposition assets (cutters, boats, aircraft, and crews) balancing force protection and post-storm operational readiness.
2. Post-storm phase:
   - Conduct lifesaving search and rescue (SAR) and flood response operations.
   - Restore the maritime transportation system.
   - Return and restore Coast Guard (CG) members, families, and facilities.
3. Throughout:
   a. Continuous operational risk management
   b. Responsible stewardship of resources
   c. Tell and document the Coast Guard story.

RADM Brown asked his team leaders to ensure that everyone gets at least one full daylight period at home, pre-storm, to ensure the readiness and safety of his or her family and home.

Leading with experience for RADM Brown meant intentionally considering not only his own experience but also the experience of his team and superiors in command. When he took command of the Seventh District just two months prior, he met with his senior leadership team but had not yet visited each of the more than eighty operational units and nine thousand active, reserve, civilian, and auxiliary CG members that comprise the district.

Despite this, he knew that his team was well-trained, well-led, and operationally ready. He was aware that different units would be at different phases of storm preparation and response at the same time, with a hurricane potentially hitting and departing Puerto Rico, producing life-threatening winds and torrential rain in the Bahamas, and being one to two days from lashing South Florida, all simultaneously. This scenario required various Coast Guard units and teams to undertake different activities under very challenging conditions, including the likelihood of power and communication outages.

For these reasons, RADM Brown chose to give enduring, overarching guidance to his subordinate commanders, without dictating specific tactics and timing. This communicated both his confidence in the technical ability of his people to perform their missions and, perhaps more importantly, confidence in their judgment and innovation in solving complex problems without micromanagement.

RADM Brown also detached most of his senior staff from their Miami headquarters, which was in the path of Hurricane Irma, to a prepared contingency command facility in St. Louis, which was exercised for this purpose previously. RADM Brown himself remained in Florida with just a few staff members to provide maximum information to the media, the public, and the hundreds of Coast Guard family members who were moved, at government expense, from vulnerable coastal areas to central Florida, again a previously planned and exercised contingency. What no one knew or could have known then was that the first week of September turned into a six-week marathon of storm response as Hurricane

Irma was quickly followed by Hurricane Maria, which devastated Puerto Rico.

The Seventh District team demonstrated exceptional success in preparing for and responding to Hurricane Irma. They performed life-saving search and rescue operations, promptly reopened closed ports (which was crucial in restarting gasoline and jet fuel supply chains for the Florida Peninsula), and returned to full operational readiness in the aftermath of the hurricane. This experience proved to be highly valuable when Hurricane Maria approached the Caribbean less than two weeks later.

Hurricane Maria ultimately struck Puerto Rico and the US Virgin Islands as a strong Category 4 hurricane, becoming the third most costly hurricane in United States history. Given that Puerto Rico is the primary hub for US Coast Guard operations in the Caribbean, the Seventh District, its subordinate Sector San Juan, and Air Station Borinquen needed to recover exceptionally quickly under extremely challenging conditions.

RADM Brown made the decision to evacuate the majority of CG-dependent family members from Puerto Rico to Florida using CG aircraft. The evacuation removed those family members from an untenable situation in which homes were damaged, power was out, communications were down, water and food were in short supply, and schools were closed. The families were brought to a hotel and conference center in South Florida that could supply their needs and provide support, including administrative, medical, and informational support. This support proved vital as communications with Puerto Rico were limited.

The evacuation of family members also allowed limited relief supplies to be focused on the uniformed Coast Guard workforce that remained in (or was sent to) Puerto Rico to perform critical missions and begin to rebuild damaged and destroyed Coast Guard facilities. Moreover, it allowed those members who remained in Puerto Rico to focus intently on their demanding workload, confident that their family members were safe, fed, and well taken care of in South Florida.

Another aspect of the hurricane response experience that proved useful during the combined Irma/Maria response period was something RADM Brown calls "horizontal leadership." This is the ability to influence and work with others without a formal leadership role or chain of command. As the smallest of the US Armed Forces, the Coast Guard often relies on and works with other agencies to perform its statutory missions. Coast Guard officers tend to learn a great deal about other agencies and entities, including their strengths, weaknesses, capabilities, and culture.

As some other agencies and local governments struggled to organize their response to Hurricane Maria, the Coast Guard convened with other Department of Homeland Security (DHS) agencies, DOD/National Guard, and local government officials at CG Air Station Borinquen. The Coast Guard and its facilities became the interagency glue that brought agencies together and helped accelerate and improve the response.

Horizontal leadership and experience proved to be beneficial two years later when Hurricane Dorian devastated the Bahamas and left them in desperate need of help. The Bahamas, which have just four hundred thousand inhabitants living on thirty of over seven hundred low-lying islands scattered across an ocean area the size of California, are especially vulnerable to hurricanes. When Hurricane Dorian stalled over the Bahamas as a Category 5 hurricane, it destroyed not only lives, infrastructure, and communications, but also the effective functioning of the Bahamian government.

At the time, RADM Brown was the Homeland Security advisor to the US President, responsible for coordinating domestic emergency response operations with state governors and the Federal Emergency Management Agency (FEMA). The Bahamas clearly needed help, but the primary coordinating agency for foreign assistance was the US Agency for International Development (USAID), an independent government agency with a different culture than FEMA or the US Coast Guard. USAID is more focused on long-term planning and contracting than immediate tactical response. Additionally, USAID is designed to respond to foreign government requests for assistance rather than to proactively engage in relief operations.

Given the circumstances, the government of the Bahamas faced challenges in assessing its needs and requesting specific support, leaving USAID and the US Department of Defense (DOD)with no actionable requests. Recognizing this dilemma, RADM Brown approached the US chargé d'affaires in the Bahamas, Lisa Johnson, with whom he had a preexisting professional relationship of mutual trust. Working together with the new Seventh Coast Guard District commander RADM Eric Jones and with the approval of the prime minister of the Bahamas, they arranged for a trained team of Coast Guard members to draft support requests on behalf of the Government of the Bahamas at the US Embassy in Nassau. These requests were written in a language and format that were easily digestible to USAID and DOD, allowing them to overcome their organizational inertia.

In conclusion, RADM Brown said, "Despite the lack of a formal organizational chart and direct chain-of-command leadership roles, the combination of shared experience, mutual understanding, and trust enabled the team to overcome organizational barriers and achieve the necessary results that both the government of the Bahamas and the United States required during this time of unprecedented challenge."

CHAPTER 1

THINKING INDEPENDENTLY

Independent thinking is a critical skill for leaders who want to succeed in today's complex and dynamic world. It enables them to embrace a diversity of thought, develop new skills, overcome barriers to independent thinking, and apply these practices to leadership. Leaders can effectively navigate ambiguity, make informed decisions, and drive innovation. They also inspire their teams to think creatively and challenge the status quo, leading to breakthrough ideas and solutions. In this chapter, we explore the importance of independent thinking for leaders and provide practical tips and strategies for developing this essential skill.

I'll share with you five categories of independent thinking:

1. The importance of independent thinking for leaders

As a leader, your decisions can have a significant impact on your team, your organization, and even your industry. Therefore, it is essential to have the ability to think independently, critically, and creatively. Independent thinking allows you to approach situations objectively, identify potential risks and opportunities, and make informed decisions that align with your values and goals.

Independent thinking helps you to challenge the status quo, question assumptions, and find new solutions to old problems. It enables you to be proactive rather than reactive, and it empowers you to make decisions that are in the best interest of your organization and your team.

2.   Embracing diversity of thought

As a leader, we must create an environment that fosters open communication and encourages the team to share their perspectives and ideas. When we embrace diversity of thought, we can leverage the knowledge and experience of your team to create innovative solutions and make informed decisions.

It is crucial to recognize that everyone has a unique perspective and approach to problem-solving and that diversity of thought can lead to better outcomes. As a leader, we must be open to feedback and willing to challenge our own assumptions to create an environment that encourages independent thinking.

3.   Developing independent thinking skills

To think independently, we must have a strong understanding of our values, goals, and priorities. We need a deep understanding of our industry, our competition, and our market.

Always be willing to ask questions, seek out new information, and challenge assumptions. Also, it's okay to take risks and make decisions based on our own judgment, rather than relying on the opinions of others.

4.   Overcoming barriers to independent thinking

There are several barriers that can hinder us, including fear of failure, groupthink, and cognitive biases. To overcome these hurdles, be willing to challenge the status quo, and seek out diverse perspectives from different people or other organizations.

It is also essential to recognize our own cognitive biases and take steps to mitigate them. For example, we can seek out alternative perspectives, gather data from multiple sources, and challenge our own assumptions.

5. Applying independent thinking to leadership

We know this is a critical skill for leaders, and it can be applied to many aspects of leadership, including decision-making, problem-solving, and innovation. As a leader, be willing to challenge the current situation, question norms, and seek out new solutions to old problems.

It's important that we create an environment that fosters independent thinking among our team members. This means encouraging open communication, embracing a diversity of thought, and recognizing and rewarding independent thinking.

Leadership doesn't always mean that you're the CEO or a high-ranking executive. In fact, leadership can be demonstrated at all levels of an organization, from first-line supervisors to individual team members. Anyone can exhibit leadership by taking ownership of their work, demonstrating initiative, and motivating others to achieve their goals.

Being a leader is not about having a formal title or position of authority, but rather about having the courage to take action and make decisions, and encouraging others to do the same. Whether you're a first-line supervisor, a team leader, or a team member, you can demonstrate leadership by setting an example, providing support and reinforcement, and taking responsibility for your own growth and development.

Overall, leadership is a mindset and a set of behaviors that can be demonstrated at all levels of an organization. By embracing this attitude in our daily work, we can all contribute to the success and growth of our organizations.

One example of a known leader who is a good independent thinker is Elon Musk, the CEO of SpaceX and Tesla. Musk is known for his innovative ideas and his willingness to challenge conventional wisdom to achieve his goals.

Musk's approach to independent thinking is reflected in his approach to innovation. He has made it a priority to take on ambitious projects that others have deemed impossible, such as creating reusable rockets for space travel and designing electric cars that are both practical and affordable.

Musk's independent thinking has also led him to prioritize sustainability and social responsibility in his business ventures. He has advocated for the use of renewable energy sources and has spoken out about the dangers of climate change, demonstrating a willingness to take a stand on important issues.

Overall, Musk's approach to independent thinking has allowed him to disrupt traditional industries and challenge established norms, leading to significant innovation and growth in his companies. His willingness to take risks and challenge the status quo has inspired others to think differently and pursue their own innovative ideas.

Another example of an independent thinker who is successful in Colorado is Brad Feld, a venture capitalist and entrepreneur based in Boulder. Feld is known for his innovative approach to investing and his focus on building sustainable, community-driven businesses.

Feld's independent thinking is reflected in his approach to venture capital. He has made it a priority to invest in companies that align with his values and that have a positive impact on their communities. He has also advocated for a more inclusive and diverse startup ecosystem, recognizing the importance of different perspectives and experiences in driving innovation.

In addition to his work in venture capital, Feld has also been a champion for the startup community in Colorado. He has cofounded several organizations focused on supporting entrepreneurs and building a strong startup ecosystem, including the Techstars startup accelerator program and the Startup Colorado initiative.

Overall, Feld's approach to independent thinking has allowed him to make a significant impact on the startup community in Colorado and beyond. His focus on building sustainable and community-driven businesses has inspired others to think differently about the role of entrepreneurship in society and has helped to create a more inclusive and diverse startup ecosystem.

In conclusion, independent thinking is a critical skill for leaders who want to make informed decisions, create innovative solutions, and lead their teams to success. By embracing diversity of thought, and overcoming barriers to independent thinking, we can become more effective and successful leaders. In the next chapter, we will discuss critical thinking. Voltaire said, "Think for yourself and let others enjoy the privilege of doing so too."

I asked our former city manager for the city of Fort Collins to give me his insight into independent leadership, and here is what he said, "Ray Lindley, Elevations Credit Union chief operating officer, recently shared powerful feedback with me about delegation, trust, and confidence: 'Do what Darin Atteberry does best and what only you can do.' In an increasingly complex environment where diverse and competing demands are commonplace, it is imperative for leaders to exercise independent critical thinking.

"When I talk with young leaders, I encourage them that when they become a city manager or a leader in general, I say, 'You and I would likely make the same decisions 90 percent of the time on most days. It's the remaining 10 percent that will differentiate us as leaders.' This is where the unique you need to be present. How you were raised, your formal education, and your lived experiences all play a role. They define you as a leader. These attributes are unique from everyone else in the room, and for that matter, from anyone else on the planet. You must be uniquely you. Along your leadership journey, many people will want you to decide just like they would. Your leadership should reflect the uniqueness of you. Don't be shy, be yourself!"

Darin Atteberry is the former city manager for the city of Fort Collins and currently works for Elevations Credit Union as the market president and SVP of government affairs and strategic relationships.

Some suggested reads to help you dive deeper:

- *Thinking, Fast and Slow* by Daniel Kahneman
- *The 7 Habits of Highly Effective People* by Stephen Convey
- *The Innovator's Dilemma* by Clayton Christensen
- *The Courage to Be Disliked* by Ichiro Kishimi and Fumitake Koga

These ladies challenge readers to think independently and develop their own beliefs and values. They are thought-provoking and empowering books that encourage readers to take responsibility for their own lives and choices.

"I could agree with you, but then we would both be wrong," said Gino Campana, a political entrepreneur. I like this statement because it implies a certain level of skepticism and critical thinking. It suggests that blindly accepting someone else's viewpoint, even if it seems agreeable at first, may lead to incorrect or misguided conclusions. This statement highlights the importance of independent thinking, intellectual integrity, and the willingness to challenge ideas in pursuit of truth.

When considering this perspective, it becomes evident that blindly conforming to another person's viewpoint can hinder personal growth and critical analysis. By acknowledging that agreement doesn't necessarily equate to correctness, one demonstrates a commitment to intellectual honesty and a desire for accurate understanding.

This statement encourages individuals to engage in active dialogue, questioning assumptions, and critically examining different perspectives. It emphasizes the significance of thoughtful reasoning and the willingness to challenge prevailing opinions. It reminds us that seeking truth requires careful evaluation and independent judgment, even if it means standing apart from popular consensus.

Ultimately, this statement promotes intellectual autonomy and the courage to hold one's ground when the prevailing opinion may not align with what one believes to be true. It serves as a reminder to be discerning and cautious when forming opinions, ensuring that they are well-founded and supported by evidence and rational thinking.

CHAPTER 2

CRITICAL THINKING

Critical thinking for leaders is the ability to analyze information, evaluate different perspectives and evidence, and make informed decisions based on logic and reason. It involves questioning traditions, identifying predispositions, and considering different viewpoints to arrive at a well-reasoned and informed decision.

Critical thinking for leaders also involves the ability to identify and solve problems, evaluate risks and opportunities, and communicate effectively with stakeholders. This skill is essential for leaders in today's complex and fast-paced business environment, where they must navigate challenging issues and make decisions that will impact the success of their organizations.

Effective leaders who possess strong critical thinking skills are better equipped to make informed decisions, innovate, and adapt to changing circumstances.

Critical thinking is a mental process that involves analyzing, synthesizing, and evaluating information. It is a systematic and disciplined approach to thinking that involves questioning assumptions, considering evidence, and evaluating arguments. This helps individuals to make knowledgeable decisions, solve problems effectively, and communicate clearly.

The process of critical thinking involves several steps, including:

1. Identify the problem or questions. The first step is to clearly define the problem or questions that need to be addressed. To identify the problem or question, it's essential to ask ourselves the following questions:

    a. What is the problem or issue that needs to be addressed?
    b. What are the key elements or factors involved in this problem?
    c. What are the causes and effects of the problem?
    d. What are the potential consequences of not solving the problem?

By answering these questions, we can gain a better understanding of the problem or question at hand, and we can begin to develop a plan for how to address it. It's also important to gather information and data to support our understanding of the problem. This can include research, data analysis, and consultation with experts or stakeholders.

Identifying a problem does not always require an extended period of time. Sometimes, emergencies arise that demand immediate critical thinking and contingency planning. I have a personal example from my teenage years that illustrates this point. A group of my friends and I used to ride the train after it picked up passengers in town, holding onto the side ladder of the cargo trailers until we could jump off. On one occasion, the train picked up speed too early, leaving us no choice but to ride it to the next town, a distance of ten miles.

Initially, we panicked and blamed each other for the dangerous situation we were in. However, we quickly realized that we needed to support one another and stay together on the same ladder. We encouraged each other to hang on and decided as a group to interlock our arms and legs to gain support. We brainstormed and kept talking to come up with other ideas or solutions. Eventually, we sensed the train slowing down and safely disembarked. The next challenge was finding our way back home.

Reflecting on this experience, I realized that we followed the essential elements of problem-solving. We identified the problem, its key elements, cause and effect, and the potential consequences of the situation. Once we calmed down, we came up with a final solution and executed it together. To prevent future crises like this, we reached a consensus and agreed not to ride the train again, and we stuck to our decision—that decision probably saved our lives.

The story of the train ride highlights an important lesson that can be applied to business crisis situations. In any crisis, whether it's a small issue that requires immediate attention or a major emergency that demands a long-term solution, the initial reaction of panic and blame is not a productive way to approach the problem.

In business, crises can arise in many different forms, from financial emergencies to public relations disasters. Whatever the nature of the crisis, the key to resolving it is to take a step back and approach it with a clear head. This means identifying the problem and its key elements, analyzing the cause and effect, and assessing the potential consequences. Just as we on the train had to work together and support each other to solve their crisis, businesses facing a crisis must also work as a team to develop a solution. This involves gathering input from various stakeholders and departments within the company, brainstorming solutions, and ultimately making a collective decision on the best course of action.

Moreover, like us teenagers who learned from our experience and made a decision not to ride the train again, businesses must also learn from their crisis and take steps to prevent it from happening again in the future. This may involve implementing new policies and procedures, improving communication and collaboration between departments, or making changes to the company's overall strategy.

Ultimately, the story of the train ride demonstrates that crises can be overcome with a combination of critical thinking, collaboration, and a willingness to learn from experience. By applying these principles to business crisis situations, companies can effectively navigate difficult times and emerge stronger and more resilient.

Once we have identified and defined the problem or question, we can move on to the next step of critical thinking, which is gathering information and data.

2. Gather information and data. Gather information from a variety of sources, including research, data, and expert opinions. Let's take a closer look at how to gather information and data for critical thinking:

    a. Identify the problem or question. This will help us determine what kind of information and data we need to gather. This may take a group brainstorming session and write them down.

    b. Determine the sources. Once we have identified the problem or question, identify the sources, which may include books, academic articles, reports, case studies, statistical data, and other credible sources.

    c. Collect the information and data. Once we have identified the sources, gather the information and data from these sources. Ensure that the information and data are reliable and accurate, and unbiased. We can take notes or use a note-taking tool to keep track of the information and data we collect.

    d. Organize the information and data. Organize them in a way that makes sense to you. You can use tables, charts, graphs, and other visual aids to help you understand the data better.

    e. Analyze the information and data. Look for developments that identify patterns, trends, and relationships that might be relevant to the problem or question. Use analytical thinking skills to assess the strengths and weaknesses of the information and data.

3. Evaluate the information and data. Use the information and data to determine their quality and relevance to the problem or question. Consider the credibility of the sources, the accuracy of the information, and the biases that may be present. Gathering information and data is an essential step in the critical thinking process. It helps us develop a comprehensive understanding of the problem or question, and it enables us to make informed decisions and develop effective solutions.

4. Consider different perspectives. Consider different perspectives and viewpoints to gain a broader understanding of the issue. This means that we need to look beyond our own beliefs, biases, and assumptions and consider alternative perspectives that may challenge or contradict our own.

Start by identifying different perspectives on the problem or issue. This may involve conducting research, talking to experts, or engaging with people who have different backgrounds, experiences, and opinions. Consider the evidence that each perspective uses to support its claims and identify any weaknesses or gaps in the reasoning.

Evaluate the strengths and weaknesses to the extent to which each perspective can explain the problem or issue in a comprehensive way. Synthesize the different perspectives by identifying commonalities and differences between them. Look for areas of agreement and disagreement and consider the implications of each perspective for addressing the problem or issue.

Developing a well-rounded understanding of an issue or problem requires considering different viewpoints. This enables you to develop a more nuanced understanding of the issue and create more effective solutions. Hopefully, it allows you to broaden your understanding of a problem or issue and to develop more comprehensive and effective solutions.

5. Communicate effectively. Communicating effectively with others includes presenting arguments and evidence in a clear and concise manner. Your communication skills don't always require high-level academic statements or explanations.

When I was on the city council and as the mayor of Fort Collins, Colorado, my strongest suggestion was a simple formula: *Simplicity equals transparency.* Complexity and ambiguity only lead to confusion. Even trial lawyers are trained to speak to a jury at a sixth to eighth-grade level. Debra Benton's book, *How to Think Like a CEO—The Vital Trials You Need to Be the Person at the Top,* is a great suggested reading about communication.

6. Use the information and data. Use what you have learned to develop informed decisions and solutions that address the problem or question. Consider the implications of your decisions and solutions and be open to revising them if new information becomes available.

Critical thinking is a skill that is developed and improved with practice. It is an essential skill for success in many areas of life, including education, business, and personal relationships. Here are two examples of critical thinkers in business leaders who were successful:

a. Mary Barra. As the CEO of General Motors (GM), Barra is known for her analytical approach to leadership and her ability to make tough decisions. She has led GM through significant changes, including the shift towards electric and autonomous vehicles, and has emphasized the importance of innovation and collaboration in driving growth.

Barra's critical thinking skills are reflected in her approach to leadership. She is a strong believer in data-driven decision-making and has made it a priority to invest in research and development to drive innovation. She is also a skilled communicator and has emphasized the importance of transparency and accountability in building trust with stakeholders.

b. Jeff Immelt. As the former CEO of General Electric (GE), Immelt is known for his strategic thinking and his ability to navigate complex business environments. He led GE through a period of significant transformation, focusing on digital innovation and the Internet of Things, and growing the company's presence in emerging markets.

Immelt's critical thinking skills are reflected in his approach to leadership. He is a strong believer in the power of innovation and has made it a priority to invest in new technologies and business models. He is also a skilled communicator and has emphasized the importance of collaboration and teamwork in driving growth and success.

Overall, the critical thinking skills of Barra and Immelt have allowed them to be successful in their respective fields. Their ability to analyze complex issues, think creatively, and develop innovative solutions has a significant impact on their organizations and on the business world.

"Education without critical thinking is like a car without a steering wheel," said Edward de Bono, a physician, author, inventor, and consultant.

Gino Campana, a political entrepreneur, noted, "It's your Camino!" This means that the individual is responsible for choosing their own path and making decisions that align with their personal goals and values. It emphasizes the importance of taking ownership of one's life and accepting the consequences of one's decisions. Essentially, it encourages people to trust their instincts, be confident in their choices, and take responsibility for their own lives.

Gino is a professional developer, entrepreneur, business leader, former council member for the city of Fort Collins, and was a candidate for the US Senate seat in Colorado.

"Remember, if you have a problem, it's your problem. Solve it. Don't blame other people. Don't burden people with your complaints. Ninety percent of the people you meet don't care about your troubles. The other 10 percent are glad you have them," stated Lou Holtz, author of *Winning Every Day: The Game Plan for Success*.

Some suggested reads to help you dive deeper:

- *The Demon-Haunted World: Science as a Candle in the Dark* by Carl Sagan. This book examines the role of critical thinking in scientific inquiry and encourages readers to be skeptical of claims that lack evidence.
- *The Righteous Mind: Why Good People are Divided by Politics and Religion* by Jonathan Haidt. This book examines the psychology of moral reasoning and how it affects our political beliefs, encouraging readers to think critically about their own values and biases.
- *The War on Normal People* by Andrew Yang. This book examines the impact of automation on the workforce and encourages critical thinking about how to address the challenges of the twenty-first-century economy.

CHAPTER 3

CREATIVE THINKING

As a leader, it is important to be able to think creatively to come up with innovative solutions to problems and to lead your team to success. Creative thinking is the ability to see things in new ways, to think outside the box, and to come up with unique solutions to challenges. In this chapter, we will discuss the importance of this exercise for leaders and provide practical tips on how to accomplish this.

Leaders who are able to think creatively have a competitive advantage in today's rapidly changing business environment. With new technologies emerging every day and globalization creating new challenges and opportunities, it is essential to think creatively to stay ahead of the curve. Innovative thinking also helps leaders to inspire their teams and come up with new and exciting ideas that can lead to growth and success.

How do you accomplish creative thinking as a leader? To encourage imaginative thinking, it is important to create a culture that values innovation and creativity. Most importantly, encourage your team members to share their ideas and provide them with opportunities to experiment and try new things. Celebrating success and failure equally can also help to create a culture where taking risks and thinking outside the box is encouraged. Remember, most colleagues are looking for opportunities to excel, and not be minimized.

1. Practice mindfulness. Mindfulness is the practice of being present in the moment and paying attention to your thoughts and feelings without judgment. This can help to quiet the mind and to create space for new ideas to emerge. By practicing mindfulness, you can become more aware of your own thought patterns and biases, which can help you break out of old ways of thinking and come up with new and innovative ideas. A couple of key factors to keep in perspective are knowing when we are wrong and getting our ego out of the way. Most people suffer burnout trying to defend what they believe is right because they let their personalities get in the way. Humbleness is OK.

2. Collaborate with others. Collaboration is a powerful tool for creative thinking. By working with others who have different perspectives and backgrounds, you can gain new insights and ideas that you may not have thought of on your own. Encourage your team members to share their ideas and to collaborate on projects to foster resourceful thinking and innovation. Those who chose not to work together are only going to be a thorn in your side and may intentionally be disruptive. So it's best to bring them in along the way and really work hard to seek their input.

3. Embrace constraints. Constraint is a great tool for creative thinking. When you are forced to work within certain limitations, you are compelled to think imaginatively to come up with solutions that work within those constraints. Embrace the limitations you face and use them to fuel your creativity.

As mayor of a community with numerous constraints, I had to juggle the competing wills and desires of the city council, the city management team, and the voters. It was like juggling three balls at the same time, wondering which one was going to drop first. To ensure that I did not drop any ball, I had to maintain constant communication with all of them. I was aware of my limitations as a leader, and I knew that the constraints were bound by law, politics, and human feelings. Therefore, I had to make sure that I kept everyone informed of the decisions being made and the rationale behind them. By doing so, I was able to balance the competing interests and ensure that the community was moving forward in a positive direction.

"America is still the land of opportunity. The only thing preventing you from being successful is you," stated Gino Campana, a political entrepreneur.

4. Take breaks. Finally, taking breaks is essential for creative thinking. When you are constantly working and focused on a task, it can be difficult to come up with new ideas. Taking a break and stepping away from your work can help to clear your mind and to create space for new ideas to emerge. That can mean taking a day off, going for a drive, exercising, and believe it or not, taking a brief nap—it clears the mind like a reset on your computer. For many years and even today, I still take power naps. Even in my office, I would close the door and lie down on the floor with my feet elevated on my chair for about twenty minutes. It's OK to do. Most of the time people don't know, and if they do, for the most part, they don't care, and they value your time.

Creative thinking is an essential skill for leaders who want to stay ahead of the curve and lead their teams to success. By creating a culture that values innovation, practicing mindfulness, collaborating with others, embracing constraints, and taking breaks, you can foster creativity and innovation within your team and achieve success in today's rapidly changing business environment.

I like what Brian Tracy said. Brian is recognized as the top sales training and personal success authority in the world today. He has authored more than sixty books and has produced more than five hundred audio and video learning programs on sales, management, business success, and personal development, including worldwide bestseller *The Psychology of Achievement*.

> The third quality of creative thinkers is that they have a willingness to change. They recognize that in a world such as ours, the unwillingness or inability to change is fatal. They prefer to be in charge of their lives rather than being caught up in the flash flood of change that is inevitable and unavoidable. The words of the truly flexible person, the person who is willing to change are simply, "I changed my mind." According to researchers, fully 70 percent of the decisions you make turn out to be wrong in the long run. This means that you must be willing to change your mind and try something else most of the time. Mental flexibility is the most important quality that you will need for success in the twenty-first century.

Here are a couple of examples of critical thinkers who are successful:

a. Richard Branson. As the founder of the Virgin Group, Branson is known for his creative approach to business and his willingness to take risks. He has built a diverse collection of companies, from airlines to music labels, and has emphasized the importance of innovation and disruption in driving growth.

Branson's creative thinking skills are reflected in his approach to entrepreneurship. He has a unique ability to identify emerging trends and develop innovative solutions to address them. He is also a skilled communicator and has emphasized the importance of brand identity and storytelling in building successful businesses.

> b. Indra Nooyi. As the former CEO of PepsiCo, Nooyi is known for her analytical approach to leadership and her ability to make tough decisions. She led PepsiCo through a period of significant transformation, focusing on healthier products and sustainable practices, and emphasizing the importance of diversity and inclusion in the workplace.

Nooyi's critical thinking skills are reflected in her approach to leadership. She is a strong believer in data-driven decision-making and has made it a priority to invest in research and development to drive innovation. She has also emphasized the importance of sustainability and corporate responsibility, recognizing that these factors are critical to long-term success in the business world.

Nooyi is also known for her ability to communicate effectively with stakeholders and build strong relationships with customers and partners. Her emphasis on transparency and accountability has helped to build trust with stakeholders and to position PepsiCo as a leader in the food and beverage industry.

Overall, Nooyi's critical thinking skills have allowed her to be successful in the business world. Her ability to analyze complex issues, think creatively, and develop innovative solutions has had a significant impact on PepsiCo and on the food and beverage industry. You will read more about her in later chapters of this book.

What is lateral thinking?

A lateral thinker is someone who uses creative and unconventional thinking to approach problems or challenges from a different angle or perspective. Lateral thinking is a term coined by Edward de Bono, a Maltese physician, author, and consultant, to describe a type of thinking that involves looking at a problem in a new way and exploring alternative solutions.

Lateral thinking involves breaking free from conventional thinking patterns and exploring new ideas, even if they seem unrelated or unconventional. It often involves combining seemingly disparate ideas or concepts to create new insights or solutions.

Lateral thinking can be useful in a variety of contexts, from problem-solving in the workplace to coming up with new creative ideas in the arts. It is often contrasted with vertical thinking, which involves a more logical and structured approach to problem-solving.

Lateral thinking is a valuable skill for anyone looking to approach problems or challenges in a new way and develop creative and innovative solutions. Sara Blakely is an example of a lateral thinker. As the founder of Spanx, Blakely is known for her creative and unconventional approach to business. She started the company with just five thousand dollars and a unique idea for women's shapewear and has since built a multi-million-dollar empire.

Blakely's lateral thinking skills are reflected in her approach to product development and marketing. She identified a gap in the market for comfortable and flattering shapewear for women and developed a unique product that met this need. She also used creative marketing tactics, such as giving away samples to Oprah Winfrey and positioning Spanx as a solution to an everyday problem faced by women.

Blakely's approach to business is also characterized by her willingness to take risks and pursue unconventional ideas. She has a reputation for challenging conventional thinking and for taking a creative approach to problem-solving and innovation.

Overall, Blakely's cross-thinking has allowed her to be successful in the business world. Her ability to identify and meet unmet needs in the market, use creative marketing tactics, and pursue unconventional ideas has had a significant impact on the fashion and apparel industry, and her success has inspired many other entrepreneurs to think creatively and take risks in their own ventures.

Overall, the creative thinking skills of these people have allowed them to be successful in their respective fields. Their ability to think outside the box, anticipate consumer needs, and develop innovative solutions has a significant impact on the tech and business industries, and their legacies continue to inspire entrepreneurs and business leaders today.

Thomas Edison once wrote, "Genius is one percent inspiration and 99 percent perspiration."

References that can help you:

- Marc Brodherson, Jason Heller, Jesk Perrey, and David Remley, *Creativity's Bottom Line: How Winning Companies Turn Creativity Into Business Value and Growth.* Accessed April 15, 2023, https://www.mckinsey.com/capabilities/mckinsey-digital/our-insights/creativitys-bottom-line-how-winning-companies-turn-creativity-into-business-value-and-growth.
- Brian Tracy, *7 Qualities of Creative Thinkers.* Accessed April 14, 2023, https://www.briantracy.com/blog/personal-success/qualities-creative-thinkers/.
- John Adair, *The Art of Creative Thinking: How to be Innovative and Develop Great Ideas* (February 24, 2009).

The last book shows you how to develop your understanding of the creative process, overcome barriers to creating new ideas, broaden your vision, build on new ideas, develop a creative attitude, and become more confident as a creative thinker.

"Creative thinking is not optional. Our world is ever-changing and unpredictable and requires creative solutions. Who saw COVID-19 coming? In an instant, our world changed and required creative thinking to navigate through it. A great leader must be nimble and use creative thinking to navigate this ever-changing world," said Luke McFetridge, principal at Noble Venture, Fort Collins, Colorado. His mission is to maximize real estate to meet the community and market demands by creating above-average returns and long-lasting relationships.

CHAPTER 4

THE ART OF PROBLEM-SOLVING

When it comes to leadership, few skills are as important as the ability to solve problems. Whether you're leading a team, a company, or a community, you'll encounter obstacles and challenges that require resourceful solutions. Unfortunately, problem-solving is often easier said than done. In this chapter, we'll explore the difficulties of problem-solving and the leadership styles and techniques that can help you overcome them.

The difficulties of problem-solving

One of the primary difficulties of problem-solving is that it can be easy to get stuck in a single mode of thinking. When faced with a problem, our brains often default to the most obvious or familiar solution, rather than considering all the possible options. This is known as a cognitive bias, and it can prevent us from finding the best solution.

Another challenge of problem-solving is that it can be emotionally draining. When you're grappling with a difficult problem, it's easy to feel frustrated, overwhelmed, or stuck. It's important to recognize these emotions and find ways to manage them, so they don't impede your problem-solving abilities.

Finally, problem-solving can be a time-consuming process. It's not uncommon to spend hours or even days working on a single problem. This can be frustrating, especially if you're working on a tight deadline.

Leadership styles for problem-solving

To be an effective problem-solver, it's important to adopt a leadership style that emphasizes collaboration and creativity. Some of the most effective leadership styles for problem-solving include:

1. Participative leadership. This style of leadership engages team members in the problem-solving process. By encouraging input from everyone on your team, you can gather a diversity of ideas and perspectives, which can lead to more innovative solutions.
2. Transformational leadership. Transformational leaders inspire and motivate their teams to work toward a common goal. By creating a shared vision and fostering a sense of teamwork, transformational leaders can help their teams overcome even the toughest problems.

An example of transformational leadership is Mahatma Gandhi, the political and spiritual leader who played a key role in India's struggle for independence from British colonial rule. Gandhi was a transformational leader who inspired and motivated people to work towards a shared vision of freedom and independence, and his leadership style has had a lasting impact on India and the world.

Gandhi's leadership style was characterized by his ability to inspire and empower people through his personal example and vision. He emphasized the importance of non-violent resistance and encouraged people to peacefully resist British rule through acts of civil disobedience. Gandhi's leadership also focused on building a sense of community and shared identity among his followers, as well as promoting social justice and equality for all people.

Gandhi's transformational leadership was evident in his ability to motivate and inspire people to take action toward a shared vision of independence and freedom. He believed in the power of individual transformation and encouraged people to cultivate qualities like self-discipline, self-sacrifice, and compassion. Through his leadership, Gandhi was able to mobilize millions of people in the struggle for independence, and his legacy continues to inspire people around the world today.

3. Servant leadership. This style of leadership emphasizes putting the needs of others first. By focusing on the needs of your team and your community, you can build trust and goodwill, which can help you navigate difficult problems.

Problem-solving techniques

In addition to adopting an effective leadership style, there are several problem-solving techniques that can help you overcome obstacles and find innovative solutions. These include:

1. Brainstorming. This technique involves generating many ideas without evaluating them. By allowing for free-flowing creativity, brainstorming can help you come up with unexpected and innovative solutions.
2. Root cause analysis. This technique entails the identification of the underlying cause of a problem, rather than simply addressing the symptoms. By addressing the root cause, one can prevent the problem from recurring in the future.

Even in community policing, law enforcement has developed the ability to uncover the fundamental reason behind a specific crime trend. The late Herman Goldstein (1931–2020), a respected professor emeritus at the University of Wisconsin-Madison Law

School and the original architect of the problem-oriented approach to policing, stressed the importance of identifying the root cause behind a series of crimes, such as a surge in homicides.

In his book *Problem-oriented Policing*, he emphasizes the significance of investigating the fundamental cause of a crime pattern. One community discovered that an increase in prostitution was the reason for their rising homicide rate, which subsequently led to the emergence of pimps, robberies, and other crimes that permeated the community. By taking targeted action against prostitution and conducting a thorough investigation, the community experienced a significant decrease in other crimes.

3. SWOT analysis. This technique involves identifying the strengths, weaknesses, opportunities, and threats of a situation. By understanding these factors, you can develop a more comprehensive understanding of the problem and identify potential solutions. Most of us have heard of this technique or have used it on occasion. However, the downside is not administering a consistent practice—hit-and-miss doesn't cut it. This technique doesn't require a lengthy process. In fact, you can use a SWOT analysis in ten minutes if you are working on an idea for a presentation at a group meeting. Your presentation will immediately recognize that you have initially processed the pros and cons with some potential solutions.

4. Bring the quiet ones to the table of discussion. If you have an introvert on your team, they generally have the best ideas and solutions when you call on them. Introverts are good to have at a meeting when it comes to problem-solving for several reasons.

First, introverts tend to be good listeners. They prefer to think before they speak and will take the time to listen to others' ideas and perspectives. This means that they are more receptive to diverse viewpoints, which leads to a more comprehensive understanding of the problem.

Secondly, introverts are often deep thinkers. They are more likely to spend time reflecting on a problem and considering multiple solutions in their heads before voicing their opinions. This means that when they do speak up, they are more likely to have thought through their ideas thoroughly and considered all the possible angles.

Thirdly, introverts often have a talent for creative problem-solving. They tend to be more comfortable with solitude, which can provide an environment for creativity to flourish. They are more likely to come up with unique solutions to problems that others may overlook.

Finally, introverts tend to be more comfortable with silence and seclusion, which can be advantageous in problem-solving. They may be less likely to be swayed by groupthink or influenced by the opinions of others in the room. Instead, they may feel more comfortable expressing their own ideas and opinions, even if they go against the prevailing group consensus.

Overall, introverts do bring unique strengths to problem-solving meetings, including active listening skills, deep thinking, creativity, and independence. By including introverts in the problem-solving process, teams can tap into a wider range of perspectives and increase their chances of finding innovative solutions.

"Assess, don't guess" is a crucial principle that emphasizes the importance of evaluating and analyzing a situation or problem thoroughly before making assumptions or decisions based on incomplete information or personal biases. When visiting a doctor for a yearly physical, we want to hear about our health condition based on data and tests that validate the doctor's opinion, not just a guesstimate.

Assessing is a comprehensive approach that relies on awareness, evaluation, data, and other relevant circumstances to make informed decisions, while guessing tends to ignore these crucial parameters, relying instead on hunches, past experiences, and unnecessary risks, which can lead to inaccurate outcomes and potentially disastrous consequences. What can often happen is that we are in a hurry to make a quick decision, so we are willing to guess and take shortcuts, which can be detrimental.

Conclusion

Problem-solving is a crucial skill for leaders in all fields. By adopting an effective leadership style and using problem-solving techniques, you can overcome obstacles and find innovative solutions to even the toughest problems. Remember to stay open-minded, manage your emotions, and never give up in the face of a challenge. With perseverance and creativity, you can solve any problem that comes your way. I believe that problem-solving is not just a skill, but a mindset. It's about finding creative solutions, being persistent, and never giving up until the problem is solved.

I remember being present and listening to Mikal Gorbachev make a profound statement while speaking at Colorado State University many years ago. He once said, words to the effect, that in a world filled with problems, winning a war with tanks is not the solution (You can't win a war with tanks). Instead, we must come together at the table, talk face-to-face, and find peaceful solutions through dialogue and compromise.

I like what JFK once said, "Let us never negotiate out of fear. But let us never fear to negotiate." I really do believe that debate looks for differences, while dialogue looks for solutions. It's important to be at the table so you are not on the menu.

"Every problem is a gift—without problems, we would not grow," said Anthony Robbins.

Here are some reading references for problem-solving that you may find useful:

- *Thinking, Fast and Slow* by Daniel Kahneman. This book explores how our brains work and the different thought processes we use when solving problems.

- *The Lean Startup* by Eric Ries. This book offers practical advice on how to solve problems in a business context by using a lean startup methodology.
- *Design Thinking: Understanding How Designers Think and Work* by Nigel Cross. This book explores the design thinking process and how it can be applied to solve problems in various fields.
- *Crucial Conversations: Tools for Talking When Stakes Are High* by Kerry Patterson, Joseph Grenny, Ron McMillan, and Al Switzler. This book offers strategies for addressing difficult conversations and conflicts that can arise during problem-solving.
- *Problem-Solving 101: A Simple Book for Smart People* by Ken Watanabe. This book offers a straightforward approach to problem-solving and provides insights into how to break down complex problems into manageable steps.
- *The Art of Possibility: Transforming Professional and Personal Life* by Rosamund Stone Zander and Benjamin Zander. This book offers insights into how to approach problem-solving with a positive and creative mindset.
- *Thinking in Systems: A Primer* by Donella H. Meadows. This book explores how systems thinking can be applied to solve complex problems in various fields.

These books offer a range of perspectives and approaches to problem-solving that can be helpful in different contexts.

"Discerning when it's appropriate to be autocratic and when it's appropriate to be collaborative. Unless you're in battle and lives depend on the decision you make in the next moment, then you probably have time to be collaborative," said John Feyen, Larimer County Sheriff's Office, Fort Collins, Colorado.

Sheriff John Feyen has an extensive background in law enforcement and was recently elected as the Larimer County Sheriff. He joined the Larimer County Sheriff's Office in 2000 and worked in various roles, including patrol deputy and lieutenant leading the investigations division. He also served as sergeant of the Wellington Squad and was appointed as the interim police chief of the Berthoud Police Department in 2013.

John led evacuation efforts during the 2012 High Park Fire and the 2013 flood. In 2019, John accepted an offer as an assistant chief with Fort Collins Police Services and served in various leadership roles. He holds a bachelor's degree in organizational leadership and development from CSU and graduated from prestigious institutions like Northwestern University School of Police Staff and Command and the Police Executive Research Forum's Senior Management Institute for Policing. Sheriff Feyen was elected to serve as the Larimer County sheriff and was sworn in on January 10, 2023.

CHAPTER 5

RESPONSIBLE LEADERSHIP

Being a leader is not just about making decisions and giving orders. It is a role that comes with a great deal of responsibility. A good leader understands this and takes their responsibilities seriously. They are aware that their actions and decisions have a direct impact on their team, their organization, and even their community. In this chapter, we will discuss the responsibilities of a good leader and how to avoid being irresponsible.

In these next four chapters (chapters 5–8), I talk about the four RARE things leaders often forget about being Responsible, Accountable, Relational, and Encouraging. So let's dive into responsibility first.

Responsibility is the obligation to take ownership of one's actions, decisions, and outcomes, and be accountable for the consequences that arise from them. It is the willingness to fulfill commitments, meet expectations, and contribute to the greater good, whether in the workplace, in personal relationships, or in society.

Taking responsibility involves acknowledging mistakes, learning from them, and making amends, when necessary, while also striving to achieve one's goals with integrity and excellence. It is a fundamental aspect of personal and professional growth and a cornerstone of a healthy and successful life. Not all jobs are equally difficult or equally critical. We can't all be heroes. But we are all important; our good work is essential. That's why the imaginative manager constantly seeks new ways to acknowledge each person's contribution.

Responsibility #1: Communication is indispensable.

One of the most crucial responsibilities of a good leader is to communicate effectively. A good leader must be able to communicate their vision, goals, and objectives clearly. They must also listen to their team members' feedback and concerns. Effective communication fosters a positive and productive work environment.

One example of a real person in a small business who communicated well is Michael Dell, the founder and CEO of Dell Technologies, a multinational technology company that specializes in computers, laptops, and other electronics. Michael Dell is known for his exceptional communication skills, which have helped him build strong relationships with his employees, customers, and investors. He has a talent for explaining complex technical concepts in simple terms and is skilled at crafting persuasive arguments and compelling messages.

Michael Dell's effective communication is seen in his keynote speeches at various technology conferences and events. In these speeches, he often speaks about the company's vision, mission, and values in a clear and concise manner. He also shares insights into the latest technology trends and explains how Dell Technologies is adapting to stay ahead of the competition.

In addition to his public speeches, Michael Dell is also known for his hands-on approach to communication within his company. He regularly interacts with employees at all levels and is always open to feedback and suggestions. He has even set up an internal social media platform that allows employees to communicate directly with him and share their thoughts and ideas.

Overall, Michael Dell's leadership and communication skills are instrumental in the success of Dell Technologies, which is a large technology company in the world today.

Resources:

- Toastmasters International. Toastmasters is an organization that helps individuals improve their public speaking and communication skills.
- *Harvard Business Review.* The *Harvard Business Review* offers articles, webinars, and podcasts on effective communication in the workplace.

Responsibility #2: Decision-making

Another important responsibility of a good leader is the ability to make sound decisions. A good leader must have the necessary knowledge and experience to make informed decisions. They must also be able to consider the long-term consequences of their decisions.

Being a responsible decision-maker realizes that it is important to consider all relevant information, weigh the pros and cons, and consider the potential impact of the decision on oneself and others. It is also essential to adhere to ethical and moral principles and to be guided by a sense of fairness, honesty, and respect. This involves being open-minded, receptive to feedback, and willing to learn from past experiences. It is also important to communicate clearly and effectively and to take responsibility for the consequences of one's decisions, whether positive or negative. Ultimately, being a responsible decision-maker requires a commitment to integrity, accountability, continuous improvement, and a willingness to make choices that align with one's values and goals.

Resources:

- The Decision Lab. The Decision Lab is a think tank that provides research and advice on decision-making.
- *The Lean Startup*. *The Lean Startup* is a book by Eric Ries that provides a framework for making decisions in a startup environment.

Responsibility #3: Team Management

A good leader is responsible for managing their team effectively. They must be able to delegate tasks, provide feedback, and motivate their team members. A good leader also ensures that their team has the necessary resources and support to accomplish their goals.

As a responsible team manager, it is important to cultivate a positive work environment that fosters collaboration, communication, and mutual respect. This involves setting clear expectations and goals for the team, providing regular feedback and support, and recognizing and rewarding individual and collective achievements. It is also essential to delegate tasks effectively, considering each team member's strengths and expertise, and to provide opportunities for professional development and growth.

As a manager, it is important to lead by example, demonstrating integrity, accountability, and a commitment to excellence and fostering a culture of transparency and open communication. This involves listening actively to feedback and concerns, addressing issues promptly and respectfully, and promoting a sense of shared ownership and responsibility. Ultimately, being a responsible team manager requires a dedication to building strong relationships, empowering team members, and creating a culture of trust, innovation, and success.

Back when I was a police sergeant, one of my officers approached me with a specific issue and sought my advice. Although he often asked me for guidance on various scenarios, I refrained from instructing him outright. Instead, I encouraged him to share his thoughts and plans with me. It turned out that nearly all of his decisions were sound and effective; he just needed the confidence and trust to act on them.

Resources:

- Gallup. Gallup is a research-based consulting company that provides advice on team management.
- *The One-Minute Manager*. *The One-Minute Manager* is a book by Ken Blanchard that provides practical advice on managing teams.

Irresponsibility and its consequences

Being an irresponsible leader can have serious consequences. It can lead to a lack of trust and respect from team members, poor morale, and even legal issues. Irresponsible leaders may also make poor decisions that have negative consequences for their organization.

One example of where a business was irresponsible is the case of the Ford Pinto. In the 1970s, the Ford Motor Company launched the Pinto, a compact car with a design flaw that caused it to explode in rear-end collisions. Ford engineers had identified the flaw during testing, but the company decided not to fix it due to the high cost of doing so.

As a result, numerous people were killed or seriously injured in Pinto accidents. In 1978, a landmark case was brought against Ford after a Pinto exploded in a rear-end collision, killing three young women and injuring another. It was revealed during the trial that Ford had conducted a cost-benefit analysis and determined that it was cheaper to pay off injury claims than to fix the design flaw.

The case brought attention to the issue of corporate responsibility and sparked widespread outrage. The Ford Motor Company was ultimately found guilty of criminal negligence and fined three million dollars. The Pinto remains a cautionary tale of corporate greed and the dangers of putting profits above people's safety.

Here are some examples of companies that have demonstrated responsibility towards both their business practices and their employees:

1. The Body Shop is a cosmetics company that is recognized for its commitment to ethical and sustainable business practices. The Body Shop has implemented numerous initiatives to reduce its environmental impact and promote fair trade and has also implemented employee-friendly policies such as flexible working arrangements and a commitment to fair wages.

2. Ben & Jerry's is an ice cream company that has been recognized for its commitment to social responsibility. Ben & Jerry's has implemented numerous initiatives to promote sustainability and social justice and has also implemented employee-friendly policies such as paid parental leave and a commitment to fair wages.

3. Costco is a wholesale retailer that has been recognized for its commitment to treating its employees well. Costco pays its employees above-average wages and benefits and has implemented policies such as a commitment to promoting from within and a focus on work-life balance.

4. Patagonia is a clothing company that has made sustainability and environmental responsibility a key part of its business model. In addition to its environmental initiatives, Patagonia has also implemented employee-friendly policies such as flexible working arrangements and on-site childcare.

5. Warby Parker is an eyewear company that is recognized for its commitment to both social responsibility and employee well-being. Warby Parker has implemented numerous initiatives to promote sustainability and has also

implemented employee-friendly policies such as unlimited paid time off and a commitment to work-life balance.

It is crucial to hold fellow colleagues and employees accountable for their work to maintain a productive and efficient work environment. When everyone takes responsibility for their work, it helps to ensure that deadlines are met, mistakes are minimized, and the quality of work is maintained. Additionally, holding others accountable for their work sends a message that everyone's contribution is valued and that there is a culture of respect and professionalism in the workplace. Ultimately, when everyone is held accountable for their work, it leads to a more positive and successful work environment for all. We will talk more about accountability in our next chapter.

Here are some best practices and tools that can be used to hold people and yourself responsible:

1. Set clear expectations. Clearly communicate what is expected of each person and provide specific details on the tasks, deadlines, and quality of work required.
2. Use a project management tool. Utilize project management software such as Asana, Trello, or Basecamp to assign tasks, set deadlines, and track progress.
3. Regular check-ins. Schedule regular check-ins with team members to review progress, discuss any challenges, and provide feedback.
4. Performance evaluations. Conduct regular performance appraisals to measure progress against goals and provide feedback on areas that need improvement.
5. Celebrate successes. Recognize and celebrate successes to reinforce positive behavior and encourage continued accountability.
6. Responsible partners. Pair team members with responsible partners to provide support and motivation and to hold each other accountable.

7. Personal productivity tools. For example, calendars, to-do lists, and time-tracking software to manage your own work to make yourself responsible—setting an example is always wise.

By implementing these best practices and utilizing these tools, you can create a culture of being responsible that promotes productivity, teamwork, and success.

Being a good leader is not easy, but it is a responsibility that must be taken seriously. Effective communication, sound decision-making, and team management are all crucial responsibilities of a good leader. By utilizing the resources available and avoiding irresponsibility, a good leader can help create a positive and productive work environment.

James Lam, a former chief risk officer (CRO), wrote an excellent article about the leadership failures that caused Silicon Valley Bank to fail. In the article, he highlights overarching problems with accountability and responsibility and offers key takeaways and questions for the full board and committees to consider.

Lam states, "The SVB failure is a disaster that could have been avoided. The SVB board had six committees, but its risk committee was the only one without a chair in 2022. Moreover, none of the risk committee members had direct risk management experience. The board of directors is ultimately responsible for the overall performance and risk management of a company."

Lam speaks to common sense. "One of the earliest lessons my father taught me was that a smart man learns from his own mistakes, a wise man learns from the mistakes of others, and a fool never learns."

I encourage you to read the entire article from the link provided below.

Lam, James. "Silicon Valley Bank: Key Takeaways and Questions for Board Risk Oversight." *NACD Boardtalk*, April 18, 2023. Accessed April 24, 1023, https://blog.nacdonline.org/posts/silicon-valley-bank-takeaways.

"Silicon Valley Bank's dramatic failure in early March was the product of mismanagement and supervisory missteps . . . Michael Barr, the Fed's vice chair for supervision appointed by President Joe Biden, said in the exhaustive probe of the March 10 collapse of SVB that myriad factors coalesced to bring down what had been the nation's seventeenth-largest bank," wrote Jeff Cox.

Cox, Jeff. "Fed report on SVB collapse faults bank's managers—and central bank regulators." CNBC, April 28, 2023. Accessed April 29, 2023, https://www.cnbc.com/2023/04/28/fed-report-on-svb-collapse-faults-banks-managers-and-central-bank-regulators.html.

"Responsibility is not a burden; it is a privilege. It is an opportunity to lead by example," said Simon Sinek, an author and leadership expert.

Lee Iacocca used to carry a little black book with tabs in it for every executive who reported to him. Every three months, he asked them to outline what they expect to accomplish in the next three months. At the end of the quarter, the executives know that they must report to the boss on how they did. Iacocca points out that it's self-disciplining and it forces self-evaluation. I like this analogy because it demonstrates Iacocca's responsibility, and he is holding his executives responsible as well.

The size of the job doesn't matter and the value placed on the job isn't relevant. To complete the project, we must realize that there are no unimportant jobs and no unimportant people. If a job weren't important, it wouldn't exist. Someone has to do it—and if it isn't done well, the company suffers.

CHAPTER 6

ACCOUNTABLE LEADERSHIP

Responsibility and accountability are related but distinct concepts. Responsibility refers to the duties and obligations that a person has in a particular role or position. It is the state or fact of being accountable or answerable for something within one's control. For example, a manager may have the responsibility to ensure that a project is completed on time and within budget.

Accountability, on the other hand, refers to the willingness of a person to accept responsibility for their actions or decisions. It involves being answerable for the outcomes of one's actions and taking ownership of the consequences. For example, if a project fails, the manager may be held accountable for the failure and may need to explain why it happened and what they will do to prevent it from happening again in the future.

In summary, responsibility is the obligation to do something, while accountability is accepting the consequences of one's actions or decisions related to that responsibility. Responsibility is a duty, while accountability is the obligation to answer for the outcome of fulfilling that duty. Accountability is often seen as a higher level of responsibility, as it involves taking ownership and being answerable for the results of one's actions.

I like to think of the two, responsibility and accountability, like a coin. They have two different sides but one cannot be without the other.

Holding myself accountable

As a good leader, it is essential to hold oneself accountable for the outcomes of one's actions and decisions. This involves being honest with oneself about one's strengths and weaknesses, taking ownership of mistakes, and learning from them to improve performance. To hold oneself accountable, a leader must:

a. Set clear goals and expectations. A good leader must set clear goals and expectations for themselves and their team. This ensures that everyone is working towards a common objective and makes it easier to hold oneself accountable for the outcomes. Larimer County Sheriff John Feyen says that "accepting the accountability when the organization falls short, but praising the efforts of others when the organization succeeds."

b. Measure performance. A good leader must measure their performance against the goals they have set. This involves tracking progress, identifying areas for improvement, creating metrics, and celebrating successes.

c. Take ownership. A good leader must take ownership of their mistakes and failures. This means acknowledging when things go wrong and taking responsibility for the consequences.

One example of a leader who took ownership of their mistakes and failures is Sara Blakely, the founder of Spanx. In the early days of her company, Blakely made a major manufacturing mistake that resulted in thousands of defective products being shipped to customers. Rather than blaming others or trying to cover up the mistake, Blakely took full responsibility for the error and immediately contacted every customer who had received a defective product to offer a replacement or refund.

Blakely's willingness to take ownership of the mistake not only helped to save her company's reputation but also earned her the trust and loyalty of her customers. Today, Spanx is a hugely successful brand that is sold in stores around the world, and Blakely is widely respected as a leader who is not afraid to admit her mistakes and learn from them.

Another example of a police chief who took ownership of their mistakes and failures is Chief Carmen Best of the Seattle Police Department. In 2020, during the protests sparked by the killing of George Floyd, Chief Best made the decision to abandon the East Precinct police station, which became a focal point for demonstrators.

However, the decision to abandon the precinct was widely criticized, and the police department faced backlash and accusations of abandoning the city's residents. Chief Best recognized that the decision was a mistake and took ownership of it, stating that she made the decision based on the safety of her officers but didn't fully consider the impact on the community.

Chief Best went on to work with community leaders to address the concerns of residents and rebuild trust between the police department and the community. Her willingness to take ownership of the mistake and work to make amends demonstrates strong leadership and a commitment to accountability.

d. Learn from mistakes: A good leader must learn from their mistakes and use them as an opportunity for growth and improvement. This involves reflecting on what went wrong, identifying the root cause, and taking action to prevent it from happening again.

There are several methodologies that can be used to identify the root cause of a problem, including:

1. Fishbone diagram. Also known as Ishikawa or cause-and-effect diagram, this tool is used to identify the potential causes of a problem by breaking it down into categories such as people, process, environment, and equipment.
2. Five whys. This technique involves asking "why" questions repeatedly until the root cause of the problem is identified. It helps to uncover the underlying causes of the problem by drilling down to the root cause.
3. Pareto chart. This tool helps to identify the most significant causes of a problem by analyzing data and presenting it in a graphical format. It helps to prioritize the causes that need addressing first.
4. Root cause analysis (RCA). This is a systematic approach to identifying the underlying causes of a problem. It involves collecting data, analyzing it, and identifying the root cause of the problem to develop effective solutions.
5. Failure mode and effects analysis (FMEA). This is a proactive approach to identifying potential failures and their causes before they occur. It helps to prevent problems by identifying and addressing the root causes of failures.

In summary, holding oneself accountable as a leader involves setting clear goals and expectations, measuring performance, taking ownership of mistakes, and learning from them. By doing so, a leader can build trust, credibility, and respect among their team and stakeholders, and create a culture of accountability and continuous improvement.

Holding others accountable

Holding others accountable with diplomacy is a crucial skill for any leader or team member. It requires a delicate balance of assertiveness and tact and can be challenging to navigate. Some good ways to hold others accountable with diplomacy include:

a. Be clear and direct. When holding others accountable, it's important to be clear and undeviating about your expectations and the consequences of not meeting them. However, this can be done in a diplomatic way by framing the conversation in a positive and constructive manner.

b. Focus on the issue, not the person. It's important to separate the issue from the person and avoid personal attacks or criticisms. Instead, focus on the specific behavior or action that needs to be addressed and provide feedback in a constructive and respectful way.

c. Listen actively. Active listening is a key component of holding others accountable with diplomacy. It shows that you are invested in finding a solution and helps to build trust and understanding.

d. Offer support. Holding others accountable doesn't mean leaving them to their own devices. Offering support and resources can help to facilitate change and ensure that everyone is working towards the same goal.

e. Follow up. Following up on commitments and holding yourself accountable can set a positive example and encourage others to do the same. It also reinforces the importance of accountability and shows that you are committed to achieving results.

What college teaches about accountability versus the business sector

College classes and the business sector may approach accountability differently, but there are some similarities and differences between the two. In college classes, accountability is often taught as a personal responsibility to meet academic requirements and achieve academic success. This typically involves completing assignments on time, attending classes regularly, and preparing for exams. In this context, accountability is more about individual performance and meeting academic expectations.

In the business sector, however, accountability is often broader and more complex. It involves taking ownership of one's actions and decisions and being answerable to stakeholders, including customers, employees, investors, and the wider community. Accountability in the business sector may include meeting financial targets, complying with regulations, ensuring ethical conduct, and delivering quality products or services. It is also about taking responsibility for mistakes and failures and learning from them to improve performance.

While accountability in both college classes and the business sector involves taking responsibility for one's actions, the focus and scope of accountability differ. In college classes, accountability is more about personal performance, while in the business sector, it is about organizational and societal impact. However, both contexts emphasize the importance of accountability for achieving success and meeting expectations.

The memory of the Italian father, Dominick Campana, speaking to his family about the importance of education during dinner time one evening has stayed with me. His wise statement, "College is fine as long as you're willing to learn when you get out," resonated with me, and I believe it holds true even today. In the real world, education goes beyond the classroom, and it is through experience that we truly learn and understand accountability.

Dominick's words remind us that education is a continuous process, and we must be willing to learn and adapt to succeed in the real world. The memory of that conversation has inspired me to continue learning and growing, even after completing my formal education. There is an old saying that a person doesn't grow old, but when that person stops growing they become old.

Dominick's kids learned well and all of them are very successful business leaders today. Their initial lessons in life came from their father who traveled from the old country as a young boy to the United States, where he succeeded in securing his citizenship and started work with a trowel and a wheel barrel as a bricklayer. One brick at a time, he became successful and was the cause of the success of the rest of the family with straight talk in difficult times. He was always honest and forthright with his kids.

Leaders need to be truthful because honesty builds trust and credibility, which are essential for effective leadership. When leaders are truthful, they are more likely to be perceived as authentic and reliable, which can inspire confidence and loyalty among their followers. Truthful leaders are also more likely to be respected and admired, which can help them to influence and motivate others to achieve common goals.

Truthfulness is also closely related to accountability because it involves taking responsibility for one's actions and decisions. When leaders are truthful, they are more likely to admit mistakes and learn from them, which can help them to improve their performance and make better decisions in the future. This willingness to be accountable can inspire others to do the same, creating a culture of accountability within the organization.

"People generally know right from wrong. They choose to do wrong," said Gino Campana, a political entrepreneur

Another great example of leadership was Mary Ontiveros from Colorado State University. The formulation and implementation of the Principles of Community at Colorado State University was spearheaded by Mary Ontiveros, the vice president for diversity. She displayed great leadership in articulating these values that are shared by the university community but had not been clearly defined in one place before.

The Principles of Community are simple yet fundamental values that every leader should embrace. It took courage to identify these core values and implement them across the university, which has approximately thirty thousand students, six thousand faculty, and staff members across four campuses in Fort Collins, Colorado.

These principles support the mission and vision of Colorado State University, which include access, research, teaching, service, and engagement. A collaborative and vibrant community is a foundation for learning, critical inquiry, and discovery. Therefore, it is the responsibility of each member of the CSU community to uphold these principles when interacting with one another and acting on behalf of the University.

The Principles of Community include inclusion, integrity, respect, service, and social justice. Each of these principles is vital to creating and nurturing an inclusive environment where everyone's identities, ideas, talents, and contributions are valued and affirmed.

Kate Jeracki's article "Principles of Community Point the Way for Shared Campus Values" provides further insight into the importance of these principles and their impact on the university community.

Although Mary Ontiveros has passed away, her legacy of leadership and contribution to the Principles of Community will endure as a living document for future leaders to follow. In 2010, Mary was named Colorado State University's first Latina vice president for diversity.

Jeracki, Kate. "Principles of Community Point the Way for Shared Campus Values." Colorado State University, January 19, 2016. Accessed May 13, 2023, https://source.colostate.edu/principles-of-community-point-the-way-for-shared-campus-values/

On the other hand, when leaders are not truthful, they can undermine their own credibility and trustworthiness, which can damage their relationships with their followers. Dishonesty can also make it difficult for leaders to hold themselves and others accountable, as it creates a culture of blame and excuses rather than responsibility and learning. The truth will set you free. Taking the blame can earn you credibility. JFK once said after the Bay of Pigs fiasco, "Success has many fathers, but failure is an orphan."

The recent $787.5 million settlement in the defamation lawsuit against Fox News demonstrates the importance of holding news agencies accountable for their reporting. This settlement sends a clear message that inaccurate and defamatory reporting will not be tolerated and that those responsible will be held accountable for their actions.

The impact of this settlement is likely to be felt not only by Fox News as an organization but also by its employees and anchor people. Going forward, Fox News may be more cautious in its reporting, and its employees may be more aware of the potential consequences of inaccurate or defamatory reporting. This increased scrutiny could impact the credibility of the network and may require a renewed focus on journalistic ethics and standards.

Ultimately, this settlement serves as a reminder that the public expects and deserves accurate and truthful reporting and that news agencies have a responsibility to uphold the highest standards of journalism.

In summary, leaders need to be truthful because it builds trust, credibility, and accountability, all of which are essential for effective leadership. When leaders are truthful, they can inspire confidence, motivate others, and create a culture of accountability within their organization.

"Fox News Settles Defamation Suit for $787.5 Million, Dominion Says." *New York Times*, April 18, 2023. Accessed April 18, 2023, https://www.nytimes.com/live/2023/04/18/business/fox-news-dominion-trial-settlement.

The CEO of New Mexico Land and Title, Jay D. Moore, was asked about what responsible leadership meant to him, and he replied, "Responsible leadership is not just for entrepreneurs, politicians, business, and religious leaders. It is important that everyone has the pride and responsibility to complete their tasks to the best of their abilities. Leaders have a greater duty to lead by example and have the responsibility for their employees, the community, and especially themselves. Respect for everyone under your charge from the janitors to the executives in the corner office is critical to the success of a company. In business, you have to deal with the ebbs and flows of the economy which is the macro aspect of the business but also the micro aspect of handling and managing the everyday issues and challenges that leaders must confront constantly.

"A responsible leader lives and owns up to their responsibilities and has the accountability to lead not only their business but the community at large. As a responsible leader you guide individual employees, and groups of employees to accomplish the goals of a company. It is very easy to recognize a leader by their actions and reactions to everyday challenges. Leadership is the responsibility of everyone in an organization not just executive management."

Jay Moore has offices throughout New Mexico and is a successful business leader for the past thirty years.

There are many resources available that teach about accountability. Here are a few good ones:

- *Crucial Accountability: Tools for Resolving Violated Expectations, Broken Commitments, and Bad Behavior* by Kerry Patterson, Joseph Grenny, Ron McMillan, and Al Switzler. This book provides practical tools and strategies for holding oneself and others accountable in various situations.
- *The Oz Principle: Getting Results Through Individual and Organizational Accountability* by Roger Connors, Tom Smith, and Craig Hickman. This book outlines a framework for personal and organizational accountability and provides real-world examples and case studies.
- *Accountability: The Key to Driving a High-Performance Culture* by Greg Bustin. This book provides a practical guide to creating a culture of accountability in organizations, including strategies for setting expectations, measuring performance, and holding people accountable.
- Online courses and seminars. There are many online courses and seminars available that teach about accountability, including those offered by organizations like Udemy, Coursera, and Skillshare. These courses may cover various topics related to accountability, including personal accountability, team accountability, and organizational accountability.

"Before you talk, listen. Before you react, think. Before you criticize, achieve. Before you spend, earn. Before you quit, try," stated a social media account called @selfsaid.

CHAPTER 7

RELATIONAL LEADERSHIP

In today's world, leadership is more important than ever. With rapid changes in technology, political tensions, and a global pandemic, people are looking for leaders who can guide them through uncertainty and chaos. And what makes a good leader? It's not just about having a vision or making decisions. It's about being relational.

Being relational means building strong relationships with the people you lead. It means being empathetic and understanding, listening to their concerns and needs, and creating a culture of trust and collaboration. This kind of leadership inspires people to work together towards a common goal, and it fosters a sense of community and belonging.

We can see examples of good leadership in the news every day. One recent example is Jacinda Ardern, the prime minister of New Zealand. When a gunman killed fifty-one people at two mosques in Christchurch in 2019, Ardern demonstrated exceptional leadership. She immediately flew to the city to comfort the victims' families and wore a hijab as a sign of respect. She also implemented strict gun control laws within weeks of the attack. Her empathetic response and decisive action brought her country together and earned her international praise.

Another example is Satya Nadella, the CEO of Microsoft. When he took over the company in 2014, Microsoft was struggling to keep up with competitors like Apple and Google. Nadella focused on creating a culture of empathy and collaboration, where employees felt valued and empowered to innovate. Under his leadership, Microsoft has become one of the most valuable companies in the world.

These examples show that being relational is not just a nice-to-have quality in a leader. It's essential for creating a positive and productive work environment, fostering innovation, and achieving success. As leaders, we should strive to build strong relationships with our team members, understand their needs and concerns, and create a culture of trust and collaboration.

Building personal relationships with business directors, supervisors, and line people is critical to effective leadership. When leaders invest time and effort into developing these relationships, they foster trust, respect, and understanding. This, in turn, creates a positive work environment where employees feel valued, supported, and motivated to do their best work.

One of the most important aspects of building personal relationships is active listening. Leaders who take the time to listen to their team members demonstrate that they value their opinions, ideas, and concerns. This helps to build trust and respect, and it also provides leaders with valuable insights into the challenges their team members face.

I attended one of the monthly Fort Collins Chamber of Commerce's "Civic Conversation Extended Where Civics and Business Meet" events on April 26, 2023. The monthly meetings are designed to bring different segments of the community together to talk about current events and how they can support each other. In this particular meeting, Darin Atteberry was emceeing a panel discussion with the various law enforcement agencies, UCHealth, and the Poudre Fire Chief in Fort Collins, Colorado. Darin said something that I thought was very relevant at the beginning of the meeting. He said, "One conversation at a time is what is going to build community." From his statement, we can extrapolate that relational leadership is all about building strong relationships with individuals through meaningful conversations. I can assure you that words matter, conversations matter, and people matter.

Relational leaders understand that building trust and respect with others takes time and effort and that it requires genuine interest and investment in others. They take the time to listen, understand, and connect with others on a personal level, which helps to build a sense of community and belonging. By focusing on one conversation at a time, relational leaders create a solid foundation of trust and respect that can lead to long-term success for themselves and their organizations.

Personal relational building

Personal relationships also help leaders to better understand the strengths, weaknesses, and aspirations of their team members. This knowledge can be used to assign tasks and projects that play to each person's strengths, provide targeted training and development opportunities, and create career paths that align with their goals.

For example, a business director who takes the time to meet regularly with their supervisors and line people can gain a better understanding of the challenges they face on a day-to-day basis. This can help them to make more informed decisions, provide the necessary resources and support, and create a culture of open communication and collaboration.

Supervisors who build personal relationships with their team members can create a positive work environment where employees feel valued and supported. For instance, a supervisor who takes the time to get to know their team members on a personal level can identify when they are struggling with a particular task or are feeling overwhelmed. Then they can provide guidance, support, and resources to help the team member succeed.

Line people who have personal relationships with their supervisors and managers are more likely to feel engaged and motivated at work. They are more likely to feel that their work is meaningful and that they are making a valuable contribution to the organization.

Building personal relationships with business directors, supervisors, and line people is a key component of effective leadership. It fosters trust, respect, and understanding, and creates a positive work environment where employees feel valued and motivated to do their best work.

Networking is legitimate and relational

Networking is a powerful tool for building business relationships and improving an individual's style of being relational. It involves connecting with people in your industry, attending events and conferences, and engaging in online communities to expand your network.

By networking, individuals can meet potential clients, partners, and mentors who can help them grow their businesses and careers. It also provides opportunities to learn from others, gain new insights, and stay up to date with industry trends.

In terms of being relational, networking allows individuals to practice active listening, empathy, and effective communication. By engaging with people from diverse backgrounds and perspectives, individuals can develop a greater understanding of different points of view and learn how to build strong relationships based on trust and respect.

From a business perspective, networking can add value to a company in many ways. It can lead to new business opportunities, partnerships, and collaborations that can help the company grow and expand its reach. It can also help to build a positive reputation for the company and its leaders, which can attract top talent and investors.

I met with an executive of a mortgage department who was talking about the importance of relationships. He had just secured a very large multi-million-dollar mortgage for a business strictly based on the relationship he built with the borrower. He knew this because another lender approached him and made the statement, "Hey, you just stole a customer from me because he knew you personally." I chuckled with him, stating, "Relationships matter!"

We can see other examples of business leaders who have successfully used networking to build relationships and add value to their companies. One recent example is Jeff Bezos, the founder and former CEO of Amazon. Bezos was known for his relentless networking, attending conferences and events, and meeting with potential clients and partners. This helped him to build strong relationships with key players in the tech industry and expand Amazon's reach.

Another example is Sheryl Sandberg, the COO of Facebook. Sandberg is a well-known advocate for women in business and has used her extensive network to promote this cause. She has built relationships with influential women in politics and business, such as Hillary Clinton and Oprah Winfrey, and has used these connections to advance her mission of empowering women in the workplace.

In today's fast-paced business world, networking has become more important than ever before. With the rise of social media and online platforms, it's easier than ever to connect with people from all over the world. Networking allows you to tap into a vast pool of knowledge and expertise, and it can help you to stay up to date with the latest trends and developments in your field.

Networking also plays a crucial role in building relationships with potential clients, partners, and investors. When you attend networking events or conferences, you have the opportunity to meet people face-to-face, develop rapport, and establish trust. This can lead to new business opportunities and partnerships that can add value to both your personal and professional life.

Some of the world's most successful business leaders have recognized the power of networking in building business relationships. Bezos has credited networking with helping him to build his business. He has said, "We see our customers as invited guests to a party, and we are the hosts. It's our job every day to make every important aspect of the customer experience a little bit better."

Sandberg has written extensively about the importance of networking and building relationships in her book *Lean In*. She has said that networking has played a critical role in her career and that it has helped her to develop new skills, gain valuable insights, and build strong relationships with her colleagues and mentors.

In conclusion, networking is a powerful tool for building business relationships and improving an individual's style of being relational. It can help to expand knowledge, develop new skills, and create opportunities for collaboration and growth. By building strong relationships with potential clients, partners, and investors, networking can add value to both your personal and professional life, as well as the company's value. Successful business leaders like Jeff Bezos and Sheryl Sandberg recognize the importance of networking and have leveraged it to achieve success in their careers. It can add value to a company by creating new opportunities for growth and expansion, and it can also enhance an individual's personal value by providing opportunities to learn, grow, and connect with others.

During my tenure of being the mayor of Fort Collins, Colorado, my strongest connections, relationships, partners, and supporters came from networking and building trust and confidence within our organization and with the community. These people became a valuable resource that helped me make sound decisions with a voice of reason.

When it comes to relationships, I believe Pastor Dary Northrop of Timberline Church expressed it best during his sermon on

April 29, 2023. He talked about the church's culture of caring for one another that they have cultivated over the years. One of the statements he made was about our attitude when entering a room: "Do our attitudes say, 'Here I am,' or 'There you are?'"

As leaders, we should prioritize the needs of others over our own, lest our egos get in the way. Wayne Dyer once described ego as *Edging God Out.*

A great example of relational leadership comes from Chris Dini, who actively forged relationships while navigating his perceived illness, despite doctors informing him that he would never fulfill his dream of becoming a firefighter. He achieved the remarkable rank of captain at Poudre Fire Authority in Fort Collins, Colorado. From the moment of his birth, Chris grappled with "transposition of the great arteries," a condition that caused his ventricles to assume reversed roles. Chris himself described it by saying, "My ventricles, basically, have switched jobs."

The doctors at Denver Children's Hospital struggled to determine the appropriate treatment for his condition. However, Chris persistently challenged their understanding of the significance of exercise. Despite the doctors' advice to restrict his activity, Chris wholeheartedly engaged in intense physical training, a decision the doctors later acknowledged as correct. Through the bond of friendship, Chris effectively imparted new knowledge to medical professionals. At the age of fifteen, Chris's aspiration to become a firefighter was met with countless rejections.

Remarkably, today the doctors collaborate with Chris at the fire department to ensure his readiness. As an adult, Chris has returned to the Denver Children's Hospital for twenty years, which he openly admits feels somewhat surreal. Nevertheless, he has cultivated a strong relationship with his doctor, who consistently responds promptly to his inquiries and willingly conducts tests whenever necessary. Chris is fully aware that his cooperation may benefit the next generation of children. A heartfelt appreciation is extended to Dr. Joseph Kay, director of the Adult Congenital Heart Disease Program.

Chris's journey highlights the significance of relational leadership. By actively building relationships, he defied the limitations imposed by his illness and achieved success in his chosen career. His ability to influence and educate doctors through friendship demonstrates the power of relational connections in driving change and inspiring others. Furthermore, his commitment to returning to the Children's Hospital and collaborating with medical professionals exemplifies relational leadership in working toward the betterment of the future for himself and future generations. Without his dedication to fostering relationships and contributing to collective well-being, Chris would not have reached the position he occupies today.

Chris, despite facing a lower pay scale and the loss of his captain rank, has made the decision to pursue a career as a Denver firefighter. After spending nineteen years with Poudre Fire Authority (PFA), he felt compelled to make this change because he firmly believes that he has more to contribute in terms of leadership, even as he works his way up from the beginning ranks once again. His determination, commitment to leading by example, and constant desire for self-improvement are ingrained in his very nature, driving him to help others along his journey. It would be a mistake not to watch the Denver Children's Hospital's YouTube clip about Chris Dini at https://youtu.be/QbJtmtuhFbg.

Mark Driscoll, retired marketing president at the First National Bank of Omaha in Colorado, said, "Effective leaders use the 'ask and listen' rule. Ask at least two questions of your team before expressing one's thoughts or opinions." Does the leader truly understand what the team needs, thinks, or wants?

Eric Thompson, founder of the Leading Edge Academy in Fort Collins, Colorado, said, "Would you follow a leader who doesn't care about you? Of course not! I believe an essential trait that an effective leader must demonstrate is *empathy*. When I think about the very best leaders I have had—the ones who had the biggest impact on me and the ones who I willingly followed—they all had the incredible ability to connect with me through empathy.

They proactively built a relationship with me by being sincerely interested in getting to know me. They knew my background and my future aspirations. They knew all about my friends and family. They even knew about my challenges and fears. Their ability to *relate* to me made me trust them without question and support their vision with enthusiasm."

Eric authored two books, *The Thrive Guide to Earning $200K Per Year in Real Estate* and *Failsafe Negotiation Scripts*.

Bibliographies:

Bezos, Jeff. Quotable Quotes. Accessed April 20, 2023, https://www.goodreads.com/quotes/794527-we-see-our-customers-as-invited-guests-to-a-party.

"Assault rifles to be banned in New Zealand in aftermath of massacre, Prime Minister announces." *CNN News*, March 21, 2019. Accessed April 20, 2023. https://www.cnn.com/2019/03/20/asia/new-zealand-christchurch-gun-ban-intl/index.html.

Malik, Nesrine. "With respect: how Jacinda Ardern showed the world what a leader should be." *The Guardian News*, March 28, 2019. Accessed April 20, 2023, https://www.theguardian.com/world/2019/mar/28/with-respect-how-jacinda-ardern-showed-the-world-what-a-leader-should-be.

"Microsoft CEO Satya Nadella attributes his success to this one trait." CNBC, February 26, 2018. Accessed April 20, 2023, https://www.cnbc.com/2018/02/26/microsoft-ceo-satya-nadella-attributes-his-success-to-this-one-trait.html.

There are many great books on networking and building relationships. Here are a few recommendations:

- *Never Eat Alone* by Keith Ferrazzi. This book is a classic in the field of networking. Ferrazzi offers practical advice on how to build relationships and expand your network, and he emphasizes the importance of generosity, authenticity, and follow-up.

- *The Art of Possibility* by Rosamund Stone Zander and Benjamin Zander. This book offers a unique perspective on networking and building relationships. It encourages readers to approach interactions with others as opportunities for creativity, collaboration, and growth.
- *How to Win Friends and Influence People* by Dale Carnegie. Although this book was first published in 1936, it remains a timeless classic on building relationships. Carnegie offers practical tips on how to communicate effectively, build trust, and influence others.
- *Give and Take* by Adam Grant. This book offers a fresh perspective on networking, emphasizing the importance of being a giver rather than a taker. Grant argues that givers ultimately achieve greater success than takers, and he offers insights into how to cultivate a giving mindset.
- *The Relationship Cure* by John Gottman. This book is focused on building strong relationships in all areas of life, including personal and professional relationships. Gottman offers practical tools and strategies for improving communication, resolving conflicts, and building trust.

These books offer valuable insights and practical advice on networking and building relationships, and they are a great place to start for anyone looking to improve their relational skills.

Here are some podcast recommendations for being relational and networking:

- *The Tim Ferriss Show.* Tim Ferriss is a well-known author and entrepreneur who interviews successful people from various fields. His guests offer insights into their own success stories and share tips on networking, building relationships, and effective communication.

- *The Jordan Harbinger Show*. Jordan Harbinger is a former Wall Street lawyer turned podcast host who interviews experts in various fields. His show covers topics such as networking, building relationships, and effective communication, and his guests offer practical tips and strategies for success.
- *The Art of Charm*. This podcast focuses on social skills, including networking, building relationships, and effective communication. The hosts offer practical tips and advice for improving your social skills and building strong relationships.
- *The Accidental Creative*. This podcast is geared towards creatives and offers insights into how to be more productive, creative, and successful. The host, Todd Henry, often discusses the importance of building relationships and networking to achieve success.
- *Entrepreneur on Fire*. This podcast features interviews with successful entrepreneurs who share their stories and offer insights into building successful businesses. Many guests discuss the importance of networking and building relationships in their own success stories.

These podcasts offer valuable insights and practical advice on being relational and networking, and they are a great resource for anyone looking to improve their relational skills.

CHAPTER 8

ENCOURAGEMENT LEADS TO SUCCESS

Encouragement is a powerful tool for leaders, and it can have a significant impact on the success of a business or organization. When leaders encourage their team members, they can foster a sense of motivation, engagement, and loyalty that can lead to increased productivity, creativity, and innovation. In this chapter, we will explore the different styles of leadership by encouragement and highlight recent stories of business leaders who have used this style to achieve success.

Leaders encourage

Leaders who use encouragement as a leadership style empower their team members to achieve their goals and reach their full potential. This style of leadership involves providing positive feedback, recognizing achievements, and offering support and guidance when needed. Encouragement can help to build a sense of trust and collaboration between team members and leaders, and it can create a positive work culture that fosters creativity, innovation, and growth.

Encouragement and compliments can be powerful motivators. When people feel appreciated and valued, they are more likely to put in extra effort and take pride in their work. This is especially true in the workplace or in a leadership role, where a little bit of encouragement can go a long way toward fostering a positive and productive environment. As a mayor and a councilman, I learned that encouraging the citizens I represented can help them feel more connected and invested in their community, leading to greater civic engagement and participation. Ultimately, taking the time to show appreciation for others can have a ripple effect that benefits everyone involved, creating a more supportive and collaborative environment for everyone.

One of many examples of what encouragement can do for a community is how we built an accessible playground for all children. When I was mayor, I was visited by a concerned person, Tiffany Harris Schierenberg, from California who pointed out that our current park system was not accessible to differently-abled children. Intrigued by her observation, I decided to take a personal visit with her to some of the parks to validate Tiffany's concern. It was then that I realized that she was right and that the statistics were staggering. Approximately 10 percent of our children did not have access to public parks other than viewing them from the sidewalk. For me, this alone countered our logo that says, "Together we are better."

Determined to make a change, I took the initiative to implement a blue-ribbon panel of community leaders to take the lead on how to accomplish this mission to design and fund a park that was accessible for all children. I reached out to Brownie McGraw, a pillar of our community, to chair the committee, as she had deep compassion for our community and children as a retired schoolteacher and principal. Brownie couldn't say no and subsequently, we developed a board of approximately ten people from the community to identify donations and fundraising events to raise the money to build our first inspirational playground.

It was no easy feat, but this group raised approximately $1.2 million from all segments of our community. I persuaded the city manager to donate a segment of a new park site that was under development for this playground. The playground was completed and accessible and today it still exists for the last fifteen years. Additionally, our future parks that were built are designed to be accessible for all children. It was a great example of how a concerned citizen can spark change, and how a community can come together to make a real difference in the lives of our children. All I had to do was encourage them and help promote the concept in many venues and speaking engagements.

Different styles of leadership by encouragement

There are several different styles of leadership by encouragement, each with its own unique approach and philosophy. Some of the most common styles include:

1. Servant leadership. This style of leadership emphasizes the importance of serving others and putting their needs first. Servant leaders encourage their team members by listening to their interests, offering support, and providing opportunities for growth and development.
2. Transformational leadership. This style of leadership focuses on inspiring and motivating team members to achieve their full potential. Transformational leaders encourage their team members by setting clear goals, providing feedback, and recognizing achievements.

Jack Welch, the former CEO of General Electric, is known for his boundaryless leadership style and emphasis on setting clear goals, providing feedback, and recognizing achievements. Welch implemented the "rank and yank" system, which encouraged competition and performance-based evaluations of employees. Under this system, employees were ranked on their performance and those in the lowest percentile were let go. This system helped to create a culture of high performance and accountability at General Electric. Overall, Welch's leadership approach focused on driving results and empowering employees to achieve their goals.

3. Authentic leadership. This style of leadership emphasizes the importance of being true to oneself and leading with integrity. Authentic leaders encourage their team members by being honest, transparent, and genuine in their interactions.

Many successful business leaders have used encouragement as a leadership style to achieve success. One recent example is Satya Nadella, the CEO of Microsoft. Nadella has emphasized the importance of empathy and encouragement in his leadership style, and he has focused on empowering his team members to be creative, innovative, and collaborative.

Another example is Doug Conant, the former CEO of Campbell Soup Company. Conant used encouragement as a leadership style to turn around the struggling company, and he focused on building a positive work culture that fostered creativity, innovation, and collaboration. He encouraged his team members by recognizing their achievements, providing support and guidance, and fostering a sense of trust and collaboration.

Encouragement can also be a powerful marketing tool for businesses. In New York, the "I Love NY" campaign is a great example of how encouragement can be used to promote a brand and create a positive image. The campaign encourages people to visit New York and experience all that the city has to offer, and it has been very successful in attracting tourists and promoting the city as a great place to live, work, and visit.

Encouragement is a powerful tool for leaders, and it can have a significant impact on the success of a business or organization. By using encouragement as a leadership style, leaders can foster a sense of motivation, engagement, and loyalty that can lead to increased productivity, creativity, and innovation. Recent stories of successful business leaders show how encouragement can be used to achieve success, and the "I Love NY" campaign is a great example of how encouragement can be used as a marketing tool. Encouragement is a simple yet powerful way to inspire and motivate others, and it should be a key part of any leader's toolkit.

Leaders can encourage themselves by setting achievable goals, celebrating small wins, practicing self-care, surrounding themselves with positive influences, and focusing on their strengths rather than their weaknesses. Encouraging oneself can help leaders to maintain a positive mindset, stay motivated, and achieve their full potential.

There are several ways that a leader can stay motivated:

1. Set clear and achievable goals: Leaders must establish clear, specific, attainable, and measurable goals for themselves and their team. By having a distinct sense of purpose and direction, leaders can remain focused and motivated. Personally, I follow the S.A.M. (Specific, Attainable, Measurable) method when setting goals. This approach involves asking yourself if the goal is specific, attainable, and measurable. Using this technique, you can track your progress along the way with a matrix that includes a timetable and a productivity report to gauge your success.

2. Celebrate small wins. Leaders can celebrate small successes by acknowledging and recognizing the progress that was made towards achieving larger goals. This can be done by publicly recognizing team members who have contributed to the success, by offering words of encouragement and praise, or by providing small incentives or rewards. It's important to make the celebration meaningful and personalized to the team and the individuals involved. Celebrating small successes not only helps to maintain motivation and momentum but also creates a positive and supportive team culture that fosters a sense of accomplishment and pride.

3. Practice self-care. Leaders should prioritize self-care by taking breaks when needed, getting enough sleep, eating healthy, and exercising regularly. Taking care of oneself can help to reduce stress and increase energy levels, which can lead to greater motivation. Yearly doctor visits for a physical are often neglected, but they also can give you a success report.

4. Surround oneself with positive influences. Leaders should surround themselves with positive influences, such as supportive colleagues, mentors, or friends. This can help to create a positive work environment and provide encouragement and motivation when needed.

Let's talk about negative people and their impact on you and the organization. This is an important topic. Being around negative people can have a bad influence on leaders for several reasons:

a. Negative people can be draining. Negative people often complain, criticize, and focus on problems rather than solutions. Being around them can be emotionally draining and can sap a leader's energy and motivation.

b. Negative people can be demotivating. Negative people can bring down the morale of a team and make it difficult for leaders to motivate their team members. Being around negative people can make it harder for leaders to maintain a positive and enthusiastic attitude.

c. Negative people can be toxic. Negative people do spread negativity and toxicity throughout an organization, which creates a toxic work environment. This leads to increased stress, conflict, and turnover, which has a negative impact on the overall success of the organization.

d. Negative people can be contagious. Being around negative people makes it easier for leaders to adopt negative attitudes and behaviors themselves. This leads to a downward spiral of negativity that is difficult to break out of.

e. Negative people can hinder creativity and innovation. Negative people are resistant to change and new ideas, which hinders creativity and innovation. Leaders who are around negative people may find it harder to encourage their team members to think outside the box and come up with new solutions.

In summary, being around negative people has a bad influence on leaders because they are draining, demotivating, toxic, contagious, and hinder creativity, and innovation. Leaders should strive to surround themselves with positive influences and create a positive work culture that fosters creativity, innovation, and growth.

Now, after all this negative reading, all you need do is turn around what was said about negative people and translate it to how positive people can change your life. For example, the last negative statement, negative people hinder creativity and innovation, can now be read as positive people help with creativity and innovation. Dr. Wayne Dyer says, "If you change the way you look at things, the things you look at change."

5. Focus on strengths. Leaders should focus on their strengths rather than their weaknesses. By recognizing their own skills and abilities, leaders can build confidence and motivation to tackle new challenges and achieve success. If you don't know how to identify your strengths and weaknesses, confide in a close friend or business partner. You should trust their honest insight, but if you cannot, why are they your confidant?

Former president Lyndon Bain Johnson was once criticized for picking Bill Moyers, a media leader in the news world, as his personal confidant in the White House. Other congressional leaders questioned why he didn't pick someone from the Senate or Congress as his personal advisor, and his response was that he could trust Bill Moyers to tell him the truth. That statement alone says a lot. A good leader wants someone who is honest with them.

By implementing these strategies, leaders can stay motivated and maintain a positive mindset, even in the face of challenges and setbacks. Don't let your perceived weaknesses hold you back.

I'll close with this great experience during a keynote speech about leadership. I was asked to speak at a leadership conference for high school students at Colorado State University on July 14, 2004, while serving as the mayor of Fort Collins. Just before I spoke, students asked a panel of community leaders several questions. One student in particular, Garrett, kept raising his hand strenuously, but he was never called on. I noticed that he was blind. Honestly, I was frustrated and filled with empathy.

So when I was called up to do the closing speech for the day, I asked Garrett what he wanted to ask. He did something different than any of the other students did. He stood up to ask his question. I was impressed with his sense of respect and daring to stand alone to face his challenge. Garrett asked me, "Will I ever be given the chance to be a leader because I am blind?" Wow, my heart sank, and you could hear a pin drop. The students and the leadership panel took their eyes off Garrett and stared at me. There was a moment when I looked back at the panel wondering if they had any profound statements. No one dared to speak, because it was a very hard question that needed an answer right then and there.

My resolve was to make sure that Garrett left this conference with something he clings to for life. How do you make that happen without too much silence? My response was this: Garrett, you are a leader and don't even realize it. Who in this room could lead a life of blindness like you are today and dare to walk in this world step by step trusting that you will make it to your next destination? You take steps of faith all day long. You are a visionary person, and you see things that no one else does. We could learn from you how to be a visionary person. Never discount yourself and realize that there are many blind people in the world today who lead with success such as politicians, Helen Keller, musicians, writers, and the list goes on.

And I shared some examples with him and the students. Garrett's response took a course of learning and understanding. His response was with so much sincerity and curiosity when he said, "I never thought of it that way." Afterward, I did meet him one on one, and we talked more. I couldn't track where Garrett is today, but I'm willing to bet he is successful and I'm sure glad I left him with some words of encouragement. I'll say it again that *if we change the way we look at things, the things we look at will change.*

Be an encourager, and you will be encouraged. Garrett's story will stick with me for a lifetime. There have been many great leaders throughout history who were blind or visually impaired. Here are a few examples:

- Louis Braille was a French educator who lost his sight at a young age. He went on to invent the braille system, which revolutionized reading and writing for blind people around the world.
- Helen Keller was an American author, activist, and lecturer who was both deaf and blind. Despite these challenges, she became a leading advocate for people with disabilities and a symbol of hope and determination.
- Jorge Luis Borges was an Argentine writer and poet who lost his sight in his fifties. Despite this setback, he continued to write and publish books until his death, becoming one of the most influential writers of the twentieth century.
- Stevie Wonder is an American singer, songwriter, and musician who was born prematurely and lost his sight shortly after birth. He went on to become one of the most successful musicians of all time, winning twenty-five Grammy Awards and selling over one hundred million records worldwide.
- José Feliciano is a Puerto Rican singer, songwriter, and musician who was born blind. He became one of the

most popular Latin music artists of the twentieth century, known for his soulful voice and guitar playing.

These leaders are just a few examples of the many blind or visually impaired individuals who have achieved great success and made significant contributions to society.

I've listed some books and podcast recommendations about being an encourager through leadership:

Books:

- *The Power of Positive Leadership* by Jon Gordon. This book offers practical tips and strategies for becoming a positive leader who encourages and inspires others.
- *The Energy Bus* by Jon Gordon. This book is a fable about a man who learns to become a positive leader and encourages his team members to be their best selves.
- *The 5 Languages of Appreciation in the Workplace* by Gary Chapman and Paul White. This book offers insights into how to show appreciation and encouragement to team members in ways that resonate with them.
- *Leaders Eat Last* by Simon Sinek. This book explores the importance of building a culture of trust, collaboration, and encouragement, and offers practical tips for becoming a more effective leader.
- *Encouraging the Heart* by James Kouzes and Barry Posner. This book is a classic in the field of leadership and offers insights into how to inspire and motivate team members through encouragement and recognition.

Podcasts:

- *The Positive Leadership Podcast* by Alex Bratty. This podcast features interviews with positive leaders from various fields who share their insights and strategies for encouraging and inspiring others.

- *Lead to Win* by Michael Hyatt. This podcast offers practical tips and strategies for becoming a more effective leader, including how to encourage and motivate team members.
- *The Action Catalyst* by Southwestern Family of Podcasts. The Action Catalyst interviews top thought leaders and experts, sharing meaningful tips and advice to help you uncover your inspiration and gain valuable insights so that you can overcome setbacks, defeat mediocrity, and reach your goals in life, business, and beyond. You can find it here: https://podcasts.apple.com/us/podcast/the-action-catalyst/id650895336?i=1000612608078
- *The Learning Leader Show* by Ryan Hawk. This podcast features interviews with successful leaders who share their insights into leadership, including how to encourage and inspire others.

These books and podcasts offer valuable insights and practical tips for becoming a more encouraging and effective leader.

"Everyone thrives differently. But everyone has a chance to thrive and succeed in an environment where the team knows the leader's primary job is to encourage them, provide them with the tools they need to be successful and hold them accountable," said Mark Driscoll, retired FNBO marketing president.

"A leader is one who rises to the call with humility and without reservation, in spite of personal cost; for the leader recognizes that true purpose extends beyond his or her accolades, but rather, to spark the flame of courage in future leaders for the betterment of all," said Ana Yelen, cofounder of Healing Warriors and past CEO for the organization (https://www.healingwarriorsprogram.org).

CHAPTER 9

INTENTIONAL LEADERSHIP

Intentional leadership is a philosophy that emphasizes purposeful action, clarity of vision, and a commitment to personal and organizational growth. It is characterized by a deep understanding of oneself, a clear vision of the future, and a focus on building strong, positive relationships with others. Intentional leadership requires a deliberate and thoughtful approach to decision-making, communication, and personal development.

Implementing intentional leadership in your business requires a commitment to personal growth and expansion. The following steps can help you become an intentional leader:

Step 1: Develop a clear vision of your personal and organizational goals. This includes identifying your values, strengths, and weaknesses, as well as setting clear objectives for yourself and your team.

Identifying your values, strengths, and weaknesses, and setting clear objectives for yourself and your team is an important step in becoming an intentional leader. Here are some processes you can use to identify these aspects of yourself:

a. Values. To identify your values, start by reflecting on what is most important to you in life. What motivates you? What gives you a sense of purpose? Make a list of your top values and prioritize them. Then think about how these values can be incorporated into your work and leadership style.

b. Strengths and weaknesses. To identify your strengths, start by taking a personality test, like the Myers-Briggs Type Indicator or the StrengthsFinder assessment. Additionally, ask colleagues, friends, and family members for feedback on what they see as your strengths. Once you have identified your strengths, think about how you can leverage them in your leadership role. Make sure you have colleagues and friends that are honest with you. An old proverb says, "Iron sharpens iron, so a friend sharpens a friend." When it comes to identifying your weaknesses, develop a plan to address them and seek out resources or support to help you develop in these areas.

c. Objectives: To set clear objectives for yourself and your team, start by identifying your long-term goals. Then break down these goals into smaller, achievable objectives. Make sure these objectives are specific, measurable, and time-bound. Additionally, involve your team members in the goal-setting process to ensure that everyone is aligned and motivated toward a shared vision.

Overall, the process of identifying your values, strengths, and weaknesses, and setting clear objectives requires reflection, self-awareness, and a willingness to seek out feedback and support from others. By taking the time to assess yourself and your team, you can become a more intentional and effective leader.

Step 2: Build strong, positive relationships with your coworkers and business partners. This involves active listening, empathy, and open communication. We talked about this in chapter 7. Take a moment to reflect on that chapter again.

Step 3: Foster a culture of learning and growth within your organization. Encourage your team members to take risks, learn from failures, and seek out new opportunities for personal and professional development. Much was said about this in chapter 8.

Developing a culture of learning and growth within an organization is essential for promoting personal and professional development among team members. Foster an environment where learning is valued and encouraged, and where team members feel comfortable seeking out new opportunities for growth and development. Here are some other suggestions:

- Encourage ongoing education and training. Provide opportunities for employees to attend conferences, workshops, and training sessions to develop new skills and knowledge.
- Foster an environment of experimentation. Encourage team members to take risks and try out new ideas, even if they might fail. Celebrate these failures as opportunities for growth and learning.
- Provide regular feedback. Give feedback to team members on their strengths and weaknesses and provide opportunities for them to give feedback to you. Receiving credible feedback from team members requires creating a culture of open communication, active listening, and trust. Leaders should encourage their team members to share their thoughts and opinions freely without fear of negative consequences. It's important to actively listen to what team members have to say, acknowledge their perspectives, and ask follow-up questions for clarification. Leaders should also be willing to receive feedback without becoming defensive or dismissive. Additionally, it's important to

follow up on feedback received, taking action to address any concerns or suggestions. By creating a culture of open communication, leaders can receive credible feedback that can help drive positive change and growth within the team and organization.

- Recognize and reward learning and growth. Celebrate successes and recognize team members who are taking risks and seeking out new opportunities for growth and development.
- Promote a culture of collaboration. Encourage teamwork and collaboration to help team members learn from each other and share knowledge and skills.
- Create a safe space for learning. Provide a supportive environment where team members feel comfortable sharing their ideas, asking questions, and taking risks without fear of judgment or retribution.
- Lead by example. As a leader, model a growth mindset by taking risks, seeking out new opportunities for learning, and being open to feedback and development.

To encourage team members to take risks and seek out new opportunities for learning from failures, consider the following methods:

- Encourage experimentation. Provide opportunities for team members to try new approaches and ideas, even if they might fail.
- Celebrate failures. Recognize and celebrate failures as opportunities for growth and learning.
- Provide support. Offer resources and support to help team members learn from their failures and develop new skills.
- Encourage self-reflection. Encourage team members to reflect on their failures and identify areas for improvement.

Overall, developing a culture of learning and growth requires a commitment to ongoing education, experimentation, feedback, and collaboration. By promoting a growth mindset and providing opportunities for learning and development, you can create a culture of continuous improvement and innovation.

Step 4: Practice self-reflection and self-awareness. Regularly assess your own performance and seek out feedback from others to identify areas for improvement. This is essential for personal and professional development. Here are some methods for achieving this goal:

- Journaling. Take time each day to reflect on your thoughts and emotions and write them down in a journal. This can help you identify patterns in your behavior and thought processes.
- Mindfulness. Practice mindfulness meditation or other mindfulness techniques to increase your awareness of the present moment and your thoughts and feelings. Yoga is certainly a good method, but sometimes being alone and quiet can help you listen to yourself.
- Self-assessment tools. Use self-assessment tools like personality tests or emotional intelligence assessments to gain insight into your strengths and areas for improvement.
- Seek feedback. Ask colleagues, friends, and family members for feedback on your performance and behavior. Be open to constructive criticism and use it to identify areas for improvement. Although it may be difficult, even feedback that is harsh and mean-spirited can offer valuable insights. These negative comments may contain small but important takeaways that you can learn from, especially when they come from people who are angry or don't like you. There's something satisfying about receiving unintentionally valuable feedback from those who don't have a favorable opinion of you.

To assess your own performance, consider the following methodology:

- Set clear goals. Identify your goals and objectives for your job or role, and create a plan to achieve them. Use the SAM method: Specific, Attainable, and Measurable.
- Track your progress. Regularly assess your progress toward your goals and identify areas where you may be falling short.
- Analyze your performance. Take a critical look at your performance and consider what you could have done differently or better.
- Identify areas for improvement. Use your self-analysis to identify areas where you can improve your performance.

To seek feedback from others to identify areas of improvement, consider the following methods:

- Be open to constructive criticism. Listen to feedback with an open mind and be willing to take action on areas for improvement.
- Use feedback to inform your development. Use feedback to identify areas where you can improve your performance and create a plan to address these areas.
- Provide feedback to others. Offer feedback to your colleagues and team members to help them improve their performance and behavior.

There are several self-assessment tools available that can help individuals gain insight into their personality, strengths, weaknesses, and areas for improvement. Here are some examples of self-assessment tools:

1. Myers-Briggs Type Indicator (MBTI) is a personality assessment tool that identifies an individual's personality

type based on their preferences in four areas: extraversion versus introversion, sensing versus intuition, thinking versus feeling, and judging versus perceiving.

2. StrengthsFinder is a tool that identifies an individual's top five strengths based on a series of questions.

3. Emotional intelligence (EQ) assessments are assessments that measure an individual's emotional intelligence, including their ability to identify, understand, and manage their emotions, as well as their ability to empathize with others.

4. DISC assessment is a tool that identifies an individual's behavioral style based on four dimensions: dominance, influence, steadiness, and conscientiousness.

5. 360-degree feedback assessment is a feedback tool that gathers feedback from multiple sources, including colleagues, supervisors, and subordinates, to provide a comprehensive view of an individual's performance and behavior. I don't always agree with this methodology because it can cause some uncomfortableness, retribution, and hurt feelings. I certainly wouldn't eliminate the idea either. It must be administered cautiously.

6. CliftonStrengths is a tool that identifies an individual's top five strengths based on a series of questions.

7. Enneagram is a personality assessment tool that identifies an individual's personality type based on nine distinct types.

These self-assessment tools can provide valuable insights into an individual's personality, strengths, weaknesses, and areas for improvement. However, it's important to remember that these assessments are not definitive and should be used in conjunction with other feedback and self-reflection methods to gain a well-rounded understanding of oneself.

To know if you are being intentional or if your business partners and coworkers are being intentional, look for the following signs:

a. Clear vision and purpose. Intentional leaders have a clear vision for themselves and their organizations, and they can articulate that vision to others.
b. Positive relationships. Intentional leaders build strong, positive relationships with others, fostering trust and respect among team members.
c. Commitment to growth. Intentional leaders are committed to personal and organizational growth, and they encourage their team members to seek out new opportunities for development.
d. Self-reflection and self-awareness. Intentional leaders regularly assess their own performance and seek out feedback from others to identify areas for improvement.

Some good books and podcasts to help with your growing and learning about being an intentional leader include:

- *The 7 Habits of Highly Effective People* by Stephen Covey
- *Leaders Eat* Last by Simon Sinek
- "How to be a leader who inspires and motivates a team," podcast by Tony Brooks
- *The Accidental Creative* podcast by Todd Henry
- *The Leadership Challenge* by James Kouzes and Barry Posner

By implementing intentional leadership, you can create a culture of growth, collaboration, and success within your organization. By focusing on personal and organizational growth, fostering positive relationships, and practicing self-reflection and self-awareness, you can become an effective and intentional leader.

"Intentional leadership is not just about achieving results; it's about empowering people to do their best work, building trust, and creating a positive impact on the world," said Michael Hyatt.

I think David Peck says it well when he writes about being realistic:

"Making a dream come true requires a leader to be realistic about expectations, resources, people, and circumstances; "situational awareness" is the aviation term for it. For leaders, that means having clear standards and milestones with which to chart our course and reasonable expectations about progress. When we hit the inevitable setback, failure, or unexpected twist, realism asks that we accept, forgive, and change direction accordingly rather than hold onto a regret or to wish or hope that things would be different. Where might a good dose of realism help you implement a better measure or a course correction? The answer to that can help you discover important clues to more-rapid progress."

David Peck wrote the book *Beyond Effective Practices in Self-aware Leadership*. He is the president of Leadership Unleashed, an executive coaching and management consulting firm.

CHAPTER 10

THOUGHTFUL LEADERSHIP

Thoughtful leadership involves purposefully considering the needs and perspectives of others in decision-making processes. It requires a focus on empathy, emotional intelligence, and ethical decision-making. This type of leadership is especially important in today's fast-paced and multifaceted business world, where leaders must navigate dynamic environments and diverse stakeholder groups.

Emotional intelligence refers to a person's ability to recognize and manage their own emotions, as well as the emotions of others. Leaders with high emotional intelligence can understand and empathize with the feelings and perspectives of their team members, communicate effectively, and build strong relationships. They can regulate their own emotions and respond appropriately to the sentiments of others, making them more effective in managing conflict, motivating their team, and creating a positive work environment. Overall, emotional intelligence is an important trait for successful leadership as it allows leaders to connect with, inspire, and lead their teams effectively.

There are several methodologies that can be used to practice thoughtful leadership. One such approach is servant leadership, which emphasizes putting the needs of others first and empowering team members to reach their full potential. Another approach is authentic leadership, which involves being true to oneself and building trust with others through transparency and openness. Mindful leadership is also a useful methodology, which involves being present at that moment and aware of one's own thoughts and emotions, as well as those of others.

To train oneself and others as thoughtful leaders, it is important to focus on developing emotional intelligence, empathy, and ethical decision-making skills. This can be done through self-reflection, coaching, and training programs. It is also important to create a culture of thoughtful leadership within the organization, where leaders are recognized and rewarded for their empathetic and ethical behavior.

Several companies and small businesses are known for their thoughtful leadership practices. For example, Patagonia is committed to sustainability and ethical manufacturing practices and has built a strong reputation for kindhearted leadership. Another example is the online shoe retailer Zappos, which empowers its employees to make decisions and provides exceptional customer service.

Thoughtful leadership can have a significant impact on organizational culture and performance. Research has shown that companies with empathetic and ethical leaders tend to have higher employee engagement, lower turnover rates, and better financial performance. Additionally, it can help build trust and loyalty among stakeholders, leading to long-term success.

Thoughtful leadership isn't about how many people serve you, but it's about how many people you serve. This leader recognizes that serving others is not a sign of weakness, but a demonstration of strength and compassion. By putting the needs and aspirations of others first, a leader can inspire and empower their team to achieve great things, creating a culture of trust, respect, and collaboration.

One example of someone who is known for putting other people first and serving others is Mahatma Gandhi. Gandhi was a political and spiritual leader in India who led the Indian independence movement against British rule. He was known for his philosophy of nonviolent resistance and for promoting social justice and equality for all people.

Throughout his life, Gandhi prioritized serving others above his own needs and desires. He lived a simple life and often practiced self-sacrifice, including fasting as a means of peaceful protest. He worked tirelessly to improve the lives of the poor and marginalized and advocated for the rights of women and members of the lower classes in Indian society.

Gandhi's commitment to serving others and promoting social justice inspired many people around the world and continues to be a powerful example of thoughtful leadership today.

Another example of a thoughtful leader in a corporation is Indra Nooyi, the former CEO of PepsiCo. Nooyi is known for her focus on sustainability and diversity, as well as her commitment to corporate social responsibility.

During her tenure at PepsiCo, Nooyi implemented several initiatives aimed at reducing the company's environmental footprint and promoting healthy lifestyles. She was also a vocal advocate for workplace diversity and was recognized for her efforts to promote women and minorities to leadership positions within the company.

In addition to her work at PepsiCo, Nooyi is a strong advocate for social justice and civic engagement. She has served on a number of nonprofit boards and has been recognized for her contributions to organizations such as the Lincoln Center for the Performing Arts and the World Economic Forum.

Overall, Nooyi's thoughtful leadership has earned her a reputation as a visionary and compassionate leader who is committed to making a positive impact on the world.

"If service is below you, leadership is beyond you." I suppose we could also say the following: "Leadership surpasses those who consider themselves too elevated for service." This quote, often attributed to various individuals without a definitive origin, carries genuine wisdom. It aligns with the biblical verse Matthew 23:11, emphasizing that true greatness and leadership are achieved by embracing the role of a servant. By acknowledging that service is not beneath them, effective leaders rise above the limitations of ego and self-importance. This mindset fosters a culture of humility, empathy, and authentic care for others, enabling them to inspire and guide with compassion and understanding.

Good leaders understand that their success is not measured solely by their own accomplishments, but also by the success of those they lead. By investing time and resources in developing other leaders or new leaders, good leaders create a culture of growth and empowerment that benefits everyone in the organization. This approach not only strengthens the organization as a whole but also creates opportunities for new ideas and perspectives to emerge, leading to greater innovation and success.

This reflects a common belief among leading experts and practitioners that investing in the development of others is a key component of effective leadership. This idea is supported by research and literature on leadership development, which emphasizes the importance of mentoring, coaching, and training programs to build leadership capacity within organizations.

One example of a leader who developed good leadership that is known today is Steve Jobs, the cofounder of Apple. Jobs is widely regarded as one of the greatest innovators and business leaders of our time, and his impact on the technology industry is legendary.

However, Jobs's legacy also includes his role in developing the leadership skills of Tim Cook, who succeeded Jobs as CEO of Apple in 2011. Cook joined Apple in 1998 and worked closely with Jobs for more than a decade, serving as the company's chief operating officer and overseeing its global supply chain and sales.

During his time at Apple, Cook learned from Jobs's leadership style and developed his own approach to leadership, which emphasizes collaboration, empathy, and a focus on social responsibility. Cook has continued to build on Jobs's legacy by leading Apple through a period of significant growth and innovation, launching new products and services, and expanding the company's reach around the world.

Overall, the relationship between Jobs and Cook serves as a powerful example of how good leaders can develop other leaders and create a legacy of success that extends beyond their own tenure. Not only is this style of leadership thoughtful, but it is also thought-provoking!

"A good leader takes a little more than his share of the blame, a little less than his share of the credit," said Arnold H. Glasow, author of *Glasow's Gloombusters*, a collection of humorous quotes and anecdotes.

Cesar Chavez said it best: "It's not about grapes or lettuce, it's about people." It really is about being better, not bitter.

Here are some resources for further reading and listening:

- *The Art of Thoughtful Leadership: How to Lead with Awareness, Empathy, and Purpose* by Mindy Gibbins-Klein
- *The Mindful Leader: Ten Principles for Bringing Out the Best in Ourselves and Others* by Michael Carroll
- *The Power of Servant Leadership* by Robert K. Greenleaf
- *The Power of Authentic Leadership: Activating the 13 Keys to Achieving Prosperity Through Authenticity* by Bill George

Podcasts:

- *The Mindful Leadership Podcast* by Mindful Leader
- *The Authentic Leadership Podcast* by Authentic Leadership Global
- *The Servant Leadership Sessions* by Stone Creek Leadership Academy

"Authentic leadership is about accepting responsibility for creating the conditions that enable others to achieve a shared purpose. It involves embracing uncertainty, addressing bias, and fostering an inclusive and supportive environment. True leaders understand that their success lies in the success of their team members and work towards empowering and developing individuals to reach their full potential," said Wade O. Troxell, PhD, mayor emeritus of the city of Fort Collins.

CHAPTER 11

LEADERSHIP THROUGH CORRECTING

As a leader, it is important to recognize that correction is a natural part of the growth and development process. When team members make mistakes or fall short of expectations, it is the leader's role to provide feedback and guidance to help them improve.

However, correction must be done in a way that is productive and constructive, rather than disruptive or demoralizing. It is important for leaders to approach correction with empathy, patience, and a focus on solutions rather than blame. I wouldn't talk to a group or individual about a correctional matter without being ready to offer a solution(s). Anyone can finger point but it's another matter of helping with solutions or ideas—it will give you more credibility.

One effective approach to correction is to identify the need for improvement in a specific behavior or outcome, and then work collaboratively with the team member to develop a plan for improvement. This approach can help to build trust and rapport with team members and can create a culture of continuous improvement and learning.

Another important aspect of effective correction is to focus on solutions rather than just pointing out someone's wrongness. By offering constructive feedback and ideas for improvement, leaders can help team members to grow and develop in a positive way, rather than just highlighting their shortcomings.

Here are some good ways to identify solutions for an individual or team for correction:

1. Listen and understand. Start by listening to the individual or team member and understanding their perspective. Ask open-ended questions to get a better sense of what happened and why and be prepared to listen without judgment.

2. Identify the root cause. Once you have a better understanding of the issue, work with the individual or team member to identify the root cause of the problem. This may involve looking at processes, systems, or other factors that contributed to the issue.

3. Brainstorm solutions. Once you have identified the root cause, work collaboratively with the individual or team member to brainstorm potential solutions. Encourage creativity and open-mindedness and be willing to consider a variety of options. I'll elaborate more on brainstorming because it is a beneficial concept:

    •   Define the problem. Clearly articulate the problem or challenge that needs to be addressed. This will help to ensure that everyone is on the same page and understands what needs to be solved.

    •   Encourage diverse perspectives. Encourage everyone in the group to share their ideas and perspectives, regardless of their position or background. This can help generate a wide range of ideas and solutions.

    •   Build on ideas. Encourage the group to build on each other's ideas and avoid dismissing ideas too quickly. This can help generate more creative and innovative solutions.

- Use visual aids. Consider using visual aids, such as whiteboards or Post-it notes, to capture ideas and make connections between them. This can help to visualize the brainstorming process and to identify patterns and themes.
- Set time limits. Set time limits for the brainstorming session to ensure that everyone stays focused and engaged. This can also help to prevent the group from getting stuck on one idea and encourage them to generate more solutions.
- Evaluate and refine ideas. After the brainstorming session, evaluate and refine the ideas generated by the group. Identify the most promising ideas and develop a strategy for implementing them.

4. Evaluate and choose a solution. Once you have a list of potential solutions, evaluate each one to determine its feasibility and effectiveness. Choose the solution that is most likely to address the root cause of the issue and lead to long-term improvement.

5. Develop an action plan. Once you have chosen a solution, work with the individual or team member to develop an action plan for implementation. This plan should include specific steps, timelines, and milestones to ensure that progress is being made.

The key to identifying solutions for correction is to approach the process in a collaborative and solution-focused way. By working with the individual or team member to understand the root cause of the issue and brainstorm potential solutions, leaders can create a culture of continuous improvement and learning that benefits everyone in the organization.

These steps don't need belaboring effort. Some individual correction can literally be done in a hallway discussion and yet, covering these five steps. Making the conversation easy can ease the mind of the person you are correcting with enthusiasm, willingness, and compliance. The approach with repeated problems is an entirely different style, and we are not talking about disciplinary action in this chapter. I've often told other colleagues that sometimes we get more done in "hallway talks" than sitting in a long meeting.

These are easy steps: Listen à identify à brainstorm à evaluate à develop à implement

Several leaders have successfully implemented this approach to correction in their organizations. For example, Jeff Bezos, the CEO of Amazon, is known for his focus on continuous improvement and innovation. He has encouraged his team to experiment and take risks, while also providing constructive feedback and guidance to help them learn and grow.

Satya Nadella, the CEO of Microsoft, has emphasized the importance of empathy and collaboration in his leadership approach. He has worked to create a culture of learning and growth, where mistakes are viewed as opportunities for improvement rather than failures.

Mary Barra, the CEO of General Motors. Barra has implemented a number of changes at GM aimed at improving the quality and safety of the company's vehicles and has emphasized the importance of continuous improvement and accountability.

One notable example of Barra's approach to correction was her response to a major safety issue involving faulty ignition switches in GM vehicles. When the issue came to light in 2014, Barra took swift action to address the problem and ensure that it doesn't happen again. She implemented a series of changes to GM's culture, processes, and leadership structure to improve quality and safety, and continues to prioritize these areas in her leadership approach.

Barra's focus on quality improvement helped rebuild GM's reputation and has earned her recognition as a thoughtful and effective leader. By taking a proactive approach to correction and emphasizing the importance of continuous improvement, she created a culture of innovation and success at GM.

Leadership correction can either hurt or help an organization, depending on the style and approach used by the leader. If correction is done in a punitive or confrontational manner, it can create a culture of fear and defensiveness that stifles innovation and creativity. This approach can lead to low morale, high turnover, and a lack of trust between leaders and team members.

On the other hand, if correction is done in a constructive and collaborative manner, it can help to create a culture of growth and learning that benefits the organization. By approaching correction with empathy, patience, and a focus on solutions rather than blame, leaders can build trust with team members and create an environment where mistakes are viewed as opportunities for improvement.

Overall, the key to effective leadership correction is to approach it in a way that promotes growth and learning, rather than fear and defensiveness. Leaders who focus on building relationships, creating a culture of collaboration, and providing constructive feedback and guidance can help their organizations to thrive and succeed.

I remember a specific incident when a principal at a charter school engaged in a confrontational argument with another staff member in the middle of the hallway, with other people and students present, all because they held differing opinions. The principal's anger escalated, and they shouted, "You're fired!" at her. It was clear to everyone witnessing the scene that the outcome was inevitable, and the school principal was ultimately dismissed from their position.

"Leadership is not about being in charge. It is about taking care of those in your charge," said Simon Sinek. I like what President Eisenhower once said, "The art of leadership is getting someone else to do something you want done because they want to do it."

Here are some resources, books, and podcasts on leadership through correction:

- *Crucial Conversations: Tools for Talking When Stakes Are High* by Kerry Patterson, Joseph Grenny, Ron McMillan, and Al Switzler. This book provides practical advice for having difficult conversations, including how to approach correction in a way that is productive and effective.

- *The Culture Code: The Secrets of Highly Successful Groups* by Daniel Coyle. This book explores the importance of culture in building successful teams, including how to create a culture of feedback and correction that promotes growth and learning.
- *Radical Candor* podcast by Kim Scott. This podcast explores the concept of radical candor, which involves giving direct feedback and correction in a way that is both compassionate and effective.
- *Leaders Eat Last* by Simon Sinek. This book explores the importance of leadership in creating a culture of trust and collaboration, including how to approach correction in a way that builds trust and promotes growth.
- *HBR IdeaCast* podcast by *Harvard Business Review*. This podcast features interviews with business leaders and experts on a variety of topics related to leadership, including how to approach correction in a way that is productive and effective.

Overall, these resources provide valuable insights and practical advice for leaders looking to approach correction in a thoughtful and effective way.

At the CUNA GAC Convention 2023 held at the Walter E. Washington Convention Center in Washington DC, I appreciated Rodney Hood's statement as speaker chairman of CUNA: "Regulations should be effective, not excessive."

Ultimately, regulations or rules that are well-crafted and thoughtfully implemented are more likely to be respected and followed, leading to greater compliance and effectiveness. Regulations and rules are necessary in any society to ensure boundaries, safety, fairness, and order. However, excessive regulations can be burdensome and impede progress. Instead, regulations should be effective and resourceful, serving their intended purpose without creating unnecessary obstacles.

Operational directives strike a balance between protecting the public and business and allowing innovation and growth. They are clear, concise, and easily understandable by those who are subject to them. When regulations are effective, they help create a level playing field for all parties involved, promoting a healthy and thriving economy. A balanced approach is key.

"Growing means continuing to learn. How will you know where to improve if no one tells you? How will your team know if you don't tell them?" said Tammy Teitscheid, chief people officer of Elevations Credit Union in Boulder, Colorado.

"Leadership comes from the ability to be empathetic and see the world through someone else's eyes. That allows you to understand their viewpoint and to better represent the people. Trust in people and commitment to democracy, freedom, and the rule of law are the hallmarks of leadership in the United States of America," said Jeni Arndt, mayor of Fort Collins, Colorado.

CHAPTER 12

EXEMPLIFYING LEADERSHIP

Leadership is a key trait that is highly valued in the professional world. It is the ability to inspire and guide others toward a common goal. Exemplifying leadership means setting an example for others to follow and displaying the qualities that make a great leader. In this chapter, we will discuss what it means to exemplify leadership, how it can be displayed in a professional way, and some methods and resources to take advantage of.

What does it mean to exemplify leadership?

Exemplifying leadership means displaying the qualities that make a great leader. These qualities include:

1. Vision means having a clear idea of where you want to go and what you want to achieve. Write your own vision statement so you can review it frequently. This means setting ambitious goals and communicating them clearly to your team, while also inspiring and motivating them to work towards achieving that vision. A strong vision can

help to align your team's efforts and guide your decision-making, even in the face of uncertainty or adversity.

And here's a sample of a short, visionary statement that a leader might write down:

Our vision is to become the leading provider of sustainable, eco-friendly products in our industry, while also promoting social responsibility and community engagement. We will achieve this by actively seeking out innovative solutions, building strong partnerships, and empowering our team members to be champions of our mission.

I find that well-thought-out visionary statements are usually very brief and to the point. Here are some great examples.

- Nike: "To bring inspiration and innovation to every athlete in the world."
- SpaceX: "To enable human exploration and settlement of Mars."
- Tesla: "To accelerate the world's transition to sustainable energy."
- Google: "To organize the world's information and make it universally accessible and useful."
- Airbnb: "To help create a world where you can belong anywhere."
- Coca-Cola: "To refresh the world in mind, body, and spirit."
- Amazon: "To be Earth's most customer-centric company."
- Patagonia: "Build the best product, cause no unnecessary harm, use business to inspire and implement solutions to the environmental crisis."

These statements are short, memorable, and easily convey the company's mission and values. They can inspire and motivate employees, customers, and stakeholders to work towards the company's vision. And, for the most part, the employees and leadership team can memorize them. It's great to speak in public about the company's vision and know it at the tip of your tongue.

2. Integrity is being honest and ethical in all your dealings.
3. Empathy is being able to understand and relate to others. Empathy plays a crucial role in the business world when assuming a leadership position. As a leader, having the ability to empathize with employees and colleagues allows for better understanding and connection. By putting themselves in others' shoes and comprehending their perspectives and emotions, leaders can make informed decisions that consider the well-being and needs of their team members.

Empathy creates a supportive and inclusive work environment, fostering trust, open communication, and collaboration. It enables leaders to address conflicts and challenges with sensitivity, while also providing constructive feedback and recognizing the achievements of their team. Ultimately, by embracing empathy, leaders can cultivate strong relationships, enhance employee engagement, and drive overall success within their organizations.

4. Confidence is believing in yourself and your abilities. Confidence in oneself and others plays a vital role in promoting psychological well-being and overall health. When individuals possess self-assurance and trust in their abilities, they are more likely to take on challenges, persevere in the face of adversity, and achieve their goals. Moreover, confidence fosters a positive mindset, leading to reduced anxiety, improved resilience, and greater overall life satisfaction.

Similarly, having faith in others cultivates strong and meaningful relationships, enhances collaboration and teamwork, and encourages mutual support and growth. By actively cultivating and nurturing confidence, both in ourselves and in others, we pave the way for personal fulfillment, healthy interactions, and a thriving social environment.

5. Accountability is taking responsibility for your actions and decisions. Accountability and responsibility are like a coin that has two different sides; one can't be without the other.
6. Adaptability is being able to change and adjust to new situations. Adaptability is a critical skill for effective leadership, as it allows you to adjust to changing circumstances and navigate unexpected challenges. By being adaptable, you can lead the team through uncertain times and find creative solutions to complex problems.

It also demonstrates your willingness to learn and grow, which can inspire and motivate the team to do the same. For example, if a project is not going according to plan, an adaptable leader may pivot their strategy, delegate tasks differently, or seek input from team members to find a new path forward.

How can leadership be displayed in a professional way?

There are several ways to display leadership in a professional way. Here are a few:

1. Lead by example. Set a good example for others to follow.
2. Encourage and inspire. Motivate and inspire others to do their best. I like what Justice Ruth Bader Ginsburg said, "Fight for the things that you care about but do it in a way that inspires others to join you."
3. Communicate effectively. Communicate clearly and effectively with others. To communicate effectively, it is important to be clear, concise, and respectful in your interactions with others. This means using simple language, actively listening to others, and showing empathy

and understanding. For example, instead of sending an email with multiple requests or questions, try scheduling a face-to-face meeting or video call where you can discuss the issues in person and ensure that everyone is on the same page. Chose the right time; timing is everything in difficult situations.

It is crucial for managers or supervisors who need to address a critical or sensitive issue, or a mistake that occurred, to approach their fellow employees directly instead of calling them into their office. By physically going to the individual, the manager demonstrates respect, empathy, and a willingness to engage in a meaningful conversation. This approach fosters a more open and comfortable environment for dialogue, where the subordinate is more likely to feel heard and understood.

Engaging in face-to-face communication allows for nonverbal cues to be observed and understood, contributing to a more comprehensive understanding of the situation. It also allows for immediate clarification and the opportunity to address any questions or concerns that may arise in real-time.

Additionally, having the conversation in the subordinate's own workspace or a neutral location can help minimize power dynamics and potential feelings of intimidation. This approach promotes a sense of equality, allowing the subordinate to feel more comfortable expressing themselves and participating in problem-solving discussions.

Overall, by choosing to approach employees or colleagues directly rather than calling them into an office, management, and supervisors create a more supportive, respectful, and conducive environment for effective communication and resolution of critical or sensitive issues.

I'll share a life lesson I learned while working as a police sergeant. One day, I received a radio call from a fellow officer who needed permission to shoot a threatening dog abandoned in a basement apartment. The dog was barking aggressively and attempting to attack, making it impossible for the officer to remove it. Instead of immediately resorting to slaying the dog, I asked the officer to hold off until I could assess the situation. Upon my arrival, I cautiously cracked open the door to the basement apartment, which triggered a violent reaction from the dog.

As I lowered myself to the dog's eye level, it became less aggressive but continued to growl. However, when I presented the dog with a leash found by a tenant upstairs, its demeanor shifted, and it became friendly, wagging its tail and body. This incident made me realize that by establishing a connection with the dog on its own level, I was able to effectively communicate and peacefully resolve the situation. This experience taught me the importance of engaging in mutual communication, even in challenging circumstances, as it can lead to better outcomes. The officer and I had some good takeaways to reflect on.

4. Foster collaboration. Encourage teamwork and collaboration. In my experience with twenty-five years of police work, teamwork and collaboration were essential for survival in crisis and critical situations. We had to work together and quickly come to agreements on how to manage incidents without jeopardizing lives. This required us to put our training skills together to identify alternative plans if the initial approach went wrong.

This methodology applies not only in law enforcement but also in a business setting or when working with different groups in the community, as seen during my time as the mayor working with council members, management teams, and special interest groups.

5. Take the initiative. Be proactive and take the lead. You know the old saying: If you are not at the table, then you are on the menu. When I was a member of the city council, I found myself in the middle of a tense stalemate between the police union and the city management team

during their yearly union arbitration. Despite being at odds, I asked them to return to the negotiating table and emphasized that we could not accept their inability to reach an agreement.

Through persistence and a focus on finding common ground, they were able to facilitate a successful outcome that addressed everyone's concerns. The alternative would have resorted to falling back on the old agreement that wasn't sustainable. Being proactive requires someone to take the lead and decide the next step.

There are several methods and resources to take advantage of when it comes to exemplifying leadership. Here are a few:

1. Attend leadership training. There are many leadership training programs available that can help you develop your skills. It's more than just attending. Collecting takeaways to implement into your daily practice will create change. Hopefully, you will journalize your notes for future reference.
2. Read books on leadership. There are many great books on leadership that can provide you with valuable insights and guidance.
3. Listen to leadership podcasts. There are many leadership podcasts available that can provide you with valuable information and inspiration.
4. Seek out a mentor. Finding a mentor who is a great leader can provide you with valuable guidance and support. Leaders require mentoring, and if you don't have one, find one quickly. This is a high priority.

You will see similar themes throughout this book, mainly because the various categories and chapter topics are interwoven with your leadership talents and skillsets. Weaving these practices into who you are will help immensely.

Exemplifying leadership at any age and stage of your career

Exemplifying leadership is not limited to a particular age or stage of your career. Anyone can be a great leader, regardless of their age or level of experience. It is about displaying the qualities that make a great leader and setting a good example for others to follow. There is an old saying by an unknown author: "Man doesn't grow old, but when a man stops growing, he becomes old."

The following young people are examples of exemplary leadership:

- Mikaila Ulmer, founder of Me & the Bees Lemonade, was just four years old when she started her lemonade company, Me & the Bees Lemonade, which uses honey instead of sugar as a sweetener. She is now a teenager, and her company has grown significantly, with her products available in stores across the United States. Ulmer is known for her ability to inspire and motivate others to take action.
- Moziah Bridges, founder of Mo's Bows started his bowtie company, Mo's Bows, when he was just nine years old. His products have been featured in major fashion magazines and he has even appeared on the television show Shark Tank. Bridges is known for his creativity and his commitment to quality, as well as his ability to speak confidently and persuasively about his brand.
- Rachel Zietz founded Gladiator Lacrosse, a company that makes high-quality lacrosse equipment when she was just thirteen years old. Her products have been featured in major sporting goods stores across the United States, and she has received numerous awards for her entrepreneurship. Zietz is known for her determination and her ability to persevere in the face of challenges, as well as her focus on innovation and quality. I encourage you to view her short YouTube video: https://youtu.be/ZHuZFHstc_8

- Alina Morse founded Zollipops, a company that makes sugar-free lollipops when she was just seven years old. Her products are now available in major retailers across the United States and she has become a role model for young entrepreneurs. Morse is known for her creativity and her commitment to promoting healthy eating habits, as well as her ability to build a strong team and brand.

A person doesn't have to be seen to exemplify leadership

Exemplifying leadership is not about being seen or heard, but about setting a good example for others to follow. It is about displaying the qualities that make a great leader and inspiring others to do their best. When others are portraying your walk, your presence isn't needed. People will know that the work of others emulates your qualities.

Some examples of exemplary leaders:

- Sheryl Sandberg, COO of Facebook, known for her focus on diversity and inclusion, her advocacy for women's leadership, and her commitment to social responsibility, is a great example of exemplifying leadership.
- Patagonia CEO, Rose Marcario, is a sustainability-focused leader who has made Patagonia one of the most environmentally conscious companies in the world. She has implemented a number of initiatives to reduce the company's carbon footprint and promote sustainable practices, while also prioritizing employee well-being and work-life balance.
- Kristina Guerrero is the founder of TurboPup, a company that makes high-quality, all-natural dog food for active dogs on the go. She is known for her passion for animals and her commitment to creating a product that meets the unique needs of active dogs. Guerrero also prioritizes

giving back, donating a portion of the company's profits to animal rescue organizations.

- Ryan Hoover is the founder of Product Hunt, a website that helps people discover and share new products. He is known for his creativity and his ability to build a strong community around his brand. Hoover also prioritizes transparency and authenticity, sharing his own failures and struggles with his audience to build trust and connection.
- Umang Dua is the cofounder of Handy, a platform that connects people with home cleaning and repair services. He is known for his focus on customer satisfaction and his ability to build a strong team culture. Dua also prioritizes innovation, constantly seeking new ways to improve and grow his business.
- Danielle Weisberg and Carly Zakin are the cofounders of The Skimm, a daily email newsletter that summarizes the day's top news stories in a fun and engaging way. They are known for their creativity and their ability to build a loyal and engaged audience. Weisberg and Zakin also prioritize diversity and inclusion, making a conscious effort to feature diverse voices and perspectives in their content.

Here are some references and podcasts that you may find helpful in your quest to exemplify leadership:

- *The 7 Habits of Highly Effective People* by Stephen Covey
- *Leaders Eat Last* by Simon Sinek
- *The Leadership Podcast* hosted by Jan Rutherford and Jim Vaselopulos
- *The EntreLeadership Podcast* hosted by Ken Coleman

In conclusion, exemplifying leadership is about setting a good model for others to follow and displaying the qualities that make a great leader. It can be exhibited in a professional way by leading by example, encouraging, and inspiring others, communicating effectively, fostering collaboration, and taking initiative. There are many methods and resources available to help you develop your leadership skills, and anyone can be a great leader regardless of age or level of experience.

"A leader is one who knows the way, goes the way, and shows the way," stated John C. Maxwell. I like John Maxwell's quote because it emphasizes the importance of leadership as a combination of knowledge, action, and example. A leader must have a clear vision of the path forward, take action to move toward that vision and set an example for others to follow. It highlights the importance of leading by example and inspiring others to follow your lead.

"The greatest leader is not necessarily the one who does the greatest things. He is the one that gets the people to do the greatest things," said US President Ronald Reagan.

"Through all the years of working in a male-dominated industry, we've learned that being empathetic, authentic, and leading by example are three of the most important attributes of being a great female leader. We cannot ask others to do that which we haven't done or aren't willing to do ourselves. We've learned that understanding the needs and concerns of our team members allows for a more productive work environment. And probably most important-don't try and be someone you're not, be your true authentic self," said Carrie Baumgart and Cindy DeGroot, CEOs and owners of Markely Motors, a family-operated and family-owned business since 1936, in Fort Collins, Colorado.

Their mission is "to make a profound impact on the lives of our clients, team members, and community by serving all with uncompromised integrity, empathy, and excellence."

CHAPTER 13

WHAT IS A PASSIONATE LEADER?

Passionate leaders are those who are deeply committed to their mission, vision, and values. They are driven by a sense of purpose and a desire to make a positive impact on the world. They inspire and motivate their team members through their own enthusiasm and energy, and they are willing to take risks and make bold decisions in pursuit of their goals.

The word passionate has its origin in the Latin word *passionem*, which means suffering or enduring. The word evolved over time to refer to intense emotions, such as love or anger, and to describe a strong enthusiasm or interest in something. The Old French word passion was used in the fourteenth century to describe intense feelings or desires, and the word passionate was first used in English in the sixteenth century to describe a person who was intensely emotional or enthusiastic. Today, the word passionate is commonly used to describe a person who is deeply committed to a particular cause or interest, and who displays a strong enthusiasm and energy towards it.

Online Entomology Dictionary. Accessed April 23, 2023, https://www.etymonline.com/word/passionate.

Being a passionate leader can be extremely helpful in many ways. It can help to create a strong organizational culture, foster a sense of teamwork and collaboration, and inspire innovation and creativity. Passionate leaders are often able to rally their team members around a shared vision, and they are able to create a sense of excitement and momentum that can lead to great achievements.

However, being too passionate can also be a hindrance to your leadership. If you become too focused on your own vision and goals, you may lose sight of the needs and perspectives of your team members. You may also become too emotionally invested in your work, leading to burnout or poor decision-making.

One example of a company with a passionate leader is Apple, under the leadership of Steve Jobs. Jobs was known for his intense passion for innovation and design, and he inspired his team members to create products that were not only functional but also beautiful and intuitive. Jobs's passion helped create a culture of creativity and excellence at Apple, and it led to many groundbreaking products that have changed the world.

On the other hand, a leader who is too passionate can also create problems for their team. For example, Elon Musk, CEO of Tesla and SpaceX, is known for his passionate and sometimes erratic behavior. While his passion has helped to inspire his team members to achieve great things, it has also led to some controversies and challenges for the company.

For example, in 2018, Musk tweeted that he was considering taking Tesla private and had secured funding for the move. This caused a surge in Tesla's stock price, but it was later revealed that Musk had not actually secured the funding and the tweet was misleading. This led to an investigation by the Securities and Exchange Commission (SEC) and a settlement that required Musk to step down as chairman of Tesla and pay a twenty-million-dollar fine.

US Security and Exchange Commission. September 29, 2018. Press release, "Elon Musk Settles SEC Fraud Charges; Tesla Charged with and Resolves Securities Law Charge." Accessed April 23, 2023, https://www.sec.gov/news/press-release/2018-226.

Similarly, Musk's passion for innovation has led to some controversy at SpaceX. In 2019, the company launched sixty Starlink satellites into orbit as part of its plan to create a global internet network. However, astronomers and other scientists expressed concerns that the satellites would interfere with astronomical observations and contribute to light pollution. Musk acknowledged these concerns and promised to take steps to address them, but the controversy highlighted the potential risks of his ambitious plans.

These examples demonstrate how Elon Musk's passion for innovation and his willingness to take risks can sometimes lead to challenges for his companies. While his passion has helped to drive his companies forward and achieve great things, it has also led to some missteps and mistakes along the way.

What about a passionate politician? Being a passionate politician carries a lot of weight because it can inspire voters to believe that you are committed to your mission and that you will work tirelessly to achieve your goals. When a politician is passionate about a particular issue or cause, they can connect with voters on an emotional level and create a sense of urgency and importance around their message. This can help to build trust and credibility with voters, who may be more likely to believe that the politician will fulfill their mission once elected.

Passionate politicians can also inspire and motivate others to get involved in the political process and work towards positive change. Ultimately, being a passionate politician can help to create a sense of momentum and energy around a particular issue or campaign, which can lead to significant progress and achievements.

To be a successful passionate leader, it is important to balance your enthusiasm with a sense of perspective and empathy. You must be able to listen to and understand the needs and concerns of your team members, and you must be willing to adjust your vision and goals as needed to ensure that everyone is aligned and motivated.

The psychology around having a lot of passion or being passionate is complex and multifaceted. Research has shown that passion is a key driver of motivation, creativity, and achievement, and it can have a positive impact on well-being and happiness. However, it can also have negative consequences, such as burnout, stress, and relationship problems.

Passion is typically defined as a strong feeling of enthusiasm or excitement towards something or someone. It can be directed towards a wide range of activities or interests, such as work, hobbies, relationships, or social causes. Passion is often characterized by intense emotions, high levels of motivation and commitment, and a sense of purpose and meaning.

One theory of passion called the Dualistic Model of Passion suggests that there are two types of passion: harmonious and obsessive. Harmonious passion is characterized by a strong interest and enjoyment in an activity or interest, but it is balanced with other aspects of life, such as relationships, health, and well-being. Obsessive passion, on the other hand, is characterized by a compulsive and uncontrollable urge to engage in an activity or interest, and it can lead to negative consequences such as burnout, stress, and conflict with others.

Overall, having a lot of passion or being passionate can be a positive force in life, as long as it is balanced with other aspects of life and does not lead to negative consequences. Passion can be a key driver of motivation, creativity, and achievement, and it can contribute to a sense of purpose and meaning in life. However, it is important to be aware of the potential risks of obsessive passion and to take steps to maintain a healthy balance in life.

Some resources about the psychology behind being passionate:

1. *The Psychology of Passion: A Dualistic Model* by Robert J. Vallerand and Nathalie Houlfort. This article presents the Dualistic Model of Passion, which proposes that there are two types of passion: harmonious and obsessive. It also

discusses the psychological and social factors that influence the development and expression of passion.

2. *Passion and Purpose: The Power of Conscious Capitalism* by John Mackey, CEO of Whole Foods Market

3. *The Art of Possibility* by Rosamund Stone Zander and Benjamin Zander. This book explores the power of passion and creativity in life and work. It provides practical tools and strategies for unlocking one's creative potential and cultivating a sense of purpose and meaning.

4. *Flow: The Psychology of Optimal Experience* by Mihaly Csikszentmihalyi. This book presents the concept of flow, which is a state of optimal experience that occurs when a person is fully engaged and immersed in an activity. It explores the psychological and emotional benefits of flow and how it can be cultivated in different areas of life.

5. *The Passion Paradox: A Guide to Going All In, Finding Success, and Discovering the Benefits of an Unbalanced Life* by Brad Stulberg and Steve Magness. This book explores the benefits and risks of passion and provides practical advice for cultivating harmonious passion and avoiding the pitfalls of obsessive passion.

These resources offer different perspectives on the psychology behind being passionate and provide practical tips and strategies for cultivating passion in oneself and others.

Some resources and podcasts that can help you become a more passionate leader include:

- *The Passionate Leader Podcast*, hosted by Dr. Christopher Washington
- *The Art of Possibility* by Rosamund Stone Zander and Benjamin Zander
- *Find Your Passion and Follow It*, a podcast by John C. Maxwell

"I think the currency of leadership is transparency. You've got to be truthful. I don't think you should be vulnerable every day, but there are moments where you've got to share your soul and conscience with people and show them who you are, and not be afraid of it," said Howard Schultz, the former CEO of Starbucks.

I had the pleasure of being appointed by the governor of Colorado to serve as a trustee for Colorado Mesa University while Tim Foster was the president of the university. His leadership style is truly remarkable. Tim had the ability to move mountains without worrying about who received the credit. His charisma and excellent rapport with staff, professors, the community, and students were unparalleled. When I inquired about his approach to leadership, Tim responded, "I have always believed that leaders lead both from in front and from behind. By that, I mean that regardless of the topic one engages with the group, collects, and analyzes information and data, and makes the decision on where to go and what to do together with them. Then a leader drives to fulfill or accomplish that vision. Former Governor John Vanderhoof once told me, 'You do the right thing for the right reason, and the politics will take care of themselves.'"

Tim Foster is the former president of Colorado Mesa University. Foster was elected to the Colorado House of Representatives in 1988 and served as majority leader from 1993 to 1996. This quote is a living example of Tim Foster's legacy: "I'm not sure what I want my legacy to be," Foster told *The Daily Sentinel* on his last day. "I guess as someone who moved the school forward—someone who helped people get the skills they needed. Because people are the most important thing. They'll do more for western Colorado than any road or bridge ever will."
https://www.gjsentinel.com/news/western_colorado/tim-fosters-tenure-as-cmu-president-comes-to-an-end/article_bc07cbae-d900-11eb-ab35-c729ad36f035.html.

Yvonne Meyers is one of the most energetic, loyal, and passionate people I know. The following is her comment about leadership:

> I feel a passionate leader is someone who "feels" their leadership. What I mean by that is they show through their words and actions their commitment to the mission and values of the organization. They show up even when it's hard. They are not afraid to admit they are wrong and will apologize to their team. They will ensure all the work is done, even doing it themselves. There is not a job too small or beneath them because the customer or the work is what drives them. They want to be good role models because they understand they are always being watched. What they do will be reflected in those they lead. They guide the organization because when they wake up every day, this is exactly where they want to be. They take their job seriously but not themselves. That way they are approachable and create teams who want to work together for the best outcomes.

Yvonne Myers is the vice president of Strategic Initiatives at the Fort Collins Area Chamber of Commerce. Also, she is the former director of health systems at Columbine Health Systems for more than two decades.

"Yvonne's dedication and commitment to Fort Collins and this region are clearly visible in her work throughout this community, including her time, experience, and volunteerism with the chamber," said Ann Hutchison, president and CEO of the Fort Collins Chamber.
https://www.coloradoan.com/story/news/2022/01/04/columbine-health-director-yvonne-myers-leaving-hired-by-fort-collins-area-chamber-of-commerce/9053581002/.

CHAPTER 14

LEADING WITH EXPERIENCE

Leading with experience is about using your past experiences to guide your present actions and decisions as a leader. Experience is a valuable asset in leadership, as it provides a wealth of knowledge, skills, and insights that can help you to navigate challenges and make effective decisions. However, it is important to learn to live with experience, to continually reflect on and learn from your past experiences, and to apply your experience in a meaningful way with a structured methodology.

To lead with experience, it is important to start by reflecting on your past experiences and identifying the key lessons and insights that you have learned. This may involve taking the time to write down your experiences, reflect on what you have learned, and identify the key skills and knowledge that you have developed over time. Once you have a clear understanding of your past experiences, you can then begin to apply them in a meaningful way with a structured methodology.

One example of a structured methodology for applying experience in leadership is the plan-do-check-act (PDCA) cycle. This cycle involves planning your actions, carrying out your plan, checking the results, and then making adjustments based on what you have learned. This approach allows you to apply your experience in a systematic way, while also allowing for ongoing learning and improvement.

Another example of a structured methodology is the Six Sigma approach. Six Sigma is a data-driven methodology that is used to improve the quality of products and services by eliminating defects and reducing variability. The methodology was developed by Motorola in the 1980s and was adopted by many other organizations.

The Six Sigma approach involves a structured process of defining, measuring, analyzing, improving, and controlling (DMAIC).

1. Define. In this phase, the problem or opportunity is identified, and a team is established to work on the project. The team defines the problem, the goals, and the scope of the project.
2. Measure. In this phase, data is collected and analyzed to establish a baseline and to identify the causes of the problem. The team collects data on the process that is causing the problem and analyzes it to identify the root causes.
3. Analyze. In this phase, the team analyzes the data to identify the most important causes of the problem. The team uses statistical tools to identify the factors that are most important and to understand how they are related to the problem.
4. Improve. In this phase, the team develops and implements solutions to address the causes of the problem. The team identifies and tests potential solutions and selects the best one.
5. Control. In this phase, the team establishes a system to monitor the process and to ensure that the improvements are sustained over time. The team develops a plan for

monitoring the process and sets up a system to track progress and make adjustments as needed.

Overall, the Six Sigma approach is a structured methodology that provides a systematic approach to problem-solving and process improvement. It is designed to help organizations improve the quality of their products and services by reducing defects and variability.

In Six Sigma, the introduction of new tools or methods, even if they could be beneficial, is technically not allowed. Total dedication across all teams is generally required in Six Sigma, making it challenging to utilize or experiment with alternative process methodologies in different areas of the organization.

In the small business world, there are many examples of experienced leaders who have used their past experiences to guide their present actions and decisions. For example, Howard Schultz, the founder and former CEO of Starbucks, had a background in sales and marketing before starting Starbucks. He used his experience in these areas to create a unique brand and customer experience that has become a hallmark of Starbucks.

Another example is Sara Blakely, the founder of Spanx, who used her experience in sales to create a new type of shapewear that has revolutionized the fashion industry. She learned from her past experiences in sales to create a product that met a real need and solved a common problem for many women.

A model of how Sara Blakely learned from her past experiences is when she faced numerous rejections while trying to secure a retail distribution deal for Spanx. Rather than letting these setbacks discourage her, she used them as opportunities for growth and learning. Blakely took each rejection as feedback and refined her approach accordingly. She reached out to potential buyers, listened to their concerns, and adjusted her pitch to address their specific needs and objections. Through a repetitious process of learning from rejections, she eventually secured her first major retail partnership. Blakely's ability to adapt, learn from failures, and persevere in the face of challenges demonstrates her ongoing learning and resilience from past experiences.

Paul Mitchell, born John Paul DeJoria, is a well-known entrepreneur and philanthropist who co-founded John Paul Mitchell Systems, a hair care company that has become a global brand. Mitchell had a difficult childhood and was homeless at one point, but he used his experiences to become a successful entrepreneur and leader.

Before starting John Paul Mitchell Systems, Mitchell worked as a door-to-door salesman, selling encyclopedias and other products. He also worked as a hairstylist and salon owner, where he learned about the hair care industry and the needs of stylists and consumers. He used his experience and knowledge to create a new type of hair care product that was high-quality, affordable, and socially responsible.

Mitchell's leadership style was characterized by a focus on innovation, creativity, and social responsibility. He believed in creating products that were both effective and environmentally friendly, and he was an early advocate for cruelty-free and sustainable practices in the beauty industry. He also believed in empowering his employees and creating a positive work culture that emphasized teamwork, respect, and personal growth.

Under Mitchell's leadership, John Paul Mitchell Systems grew into a global brand with a reputation for high-quality, innovative hair care products. Paul Mitchell's experience in sales, hairstyling, and entrepreneurship helped to shape his leadership style and his approach to business. He used his past experiences to create a unique brand and a successful company that continues to be a leader in the beauty industry.

A well-known business leader quote about experience leadership comes from Peter Drucker, the father of modern management and an author, who said, "The only source of knowledge is experience." His quote emphasizes the importance of experience as a valuable source of knowledge and insight in leadership. It suggests that leaders who are able to draw on their past experiences are better equipped to make effective decisions and achieve their goals.

During my time as mayor of the city of Fort Collins, I had the opportunity to be part of the hiring process of our City Manager, Darin Atteberry, in 2005. My opportunity to work with Darin was not only a great experience but it was intriguing to watch him grow rapidly in one of the fastest-growing communities in the state of Colorado. His ability to adapt, critically analyze, and manage an organization of about two thousand employees, a council of seven, and a community of about 140,000 people was remarkable.

After leaving office in 2005, I returned to the city council in 2015 for another four-year service. The magnitude of change and improvement in the quality of service was exponential. Without going into the details, it's without a doubt that his success was greatly attributed to the experience he developed along the way. Naturally, this took a lot of teamwork, skilled communication, political juggling, and adapting to change. He has since left the city of Fort Collins at the peak of his career and now serves as an executive for Elevations Credit Union. Darin often teaches management skills throughout the United States, sharing his experiences.

Some helpful resources for leading with experience include:

- *The Experience Economy* by Joseph Pine and James Gilmore
- *The Power of Experience: How to Build Your Brand and Drive Business Results* by Kerry Bodine and Ed Bodine
- *The Art of Possibility* by Rosamund Stone Zander and Benjamin Zander

Warren Bennis said, "Leadership is the capacity to translate vision into reality, through the experience of others." This quote emphasizes the importance of experience in leadership, and the need to use that experience to create a shared vision and inspire others to achieve it.

CHAPTER 15

WHO GETS THE CREDIT?

I remember listening to Chad Holiday speak at a conference in St. Louis, Missouri. Chad, who used to be the CEO of Dupont, said while speaking to hundreds of college students that he used to tell his employees that "you can accomplish anything you want as long as you don't care who gets the credit." In our society today, some people are willing to step on others just so they can get the credit for something they may have contributed little or nothing to. Some are motivated to take drastic acts like this in hopes of a promotion or are looking for quick-fix fame.

Credits are earned and not given, and they are recognized by others who see the direct impact you have on their work environment or personal lives. Good leaders know that success is not achieved alone. It is a team effort that requires collaboration and dedication from all members. However, in some cases, leaders may be tempted to take credit for the success of their team, failing to recognize the hard work of others. This can lead to resentment and a lack of motivation among team members. Therefore, it is important for leaders to know how to give credit to others and not just themselves.

One ideal way of giving credit and recognition is to publicly acknowledge the contributions of team members. This can be done through team meetings, emails, or even social media posts. By highlighting the hard work of others, leaders can show their team members that their efforts are valued and appreciated.

Another effective way of giving credit is to provide opportunities for team members to showcase their skills and achievements. You can do this through presentations, promotions, or even awards. By doing so, leaders demonstrate their confidence in their team members and provide them with a sense of pride and accomplishment.

Giving compliments is an effective way for leaders to show appreciation for their employees and boost their morale. Here is a good methodology for leaders to give compliments to their employees face-to-face:

1. Be specific. When giving compliments, it's important to be specific about what you are praising. Instead of saying "Good job," try saying, "I really appreciate the way you handled that difficult situation with the client. Your patience and professionalism were impressive."

2. Be timely. Compliments are most effective when given soon after the achievement. Don't wait too long to give a compliment or it may lose its impact.

3. Be sincere. Compliments should come from the heart. Be genuine in your praise and avoid insincere flattery.

4. Be personal. Tailor your compliment to the individual. Everyone likes to feel recognized for their unique contributions, so make sure your compliment is personalized to the employee and their specific achievement.

5. Be private. In some cases, employees may feel uncomfortable receiving compliments in front of their colleagues. If this is the case, consider giving the compliment in private. I believe the private conversations generate more exchange and enable you to learn more about the colleague.

6. Be consistent: Compliments should be given regularly and consistently, not just when there is a major achievement. This helps to create a positive work environment and encourages employees to continue to perform well.

When approaching an employee to give a compliment, it's important to be respectful and considerate of their time and workload. Schedule a time to speak with them one-on-one, and let them know that you want to recognize their efforts and achievements. This shows that you value their contributions and that you are invested in their success.

An example of a leader who excels at complementing and rewarding their team members is John Lee Dumas, the founder of Entrepreneur on Fire. In his podcast, John regularly highlights the achievements of his team members and offers them opportunities for growth and development. He also fosters a positive work environment by encouraging open communication and collaboration, and by recognizing the unique strengths and talents of each team member.

In summary, a good approach for leaders to give compliments to their employees includes being specific, timely, sincere, personal, private (if necessary), and consistent. By approaching employees with respect and consideration, leaders can boost morale and create a positive work environment.

How do we compliment teams?

Here are the best practices for a leader to compliment a work team for their excellence or performance. In addition to what we mentioned earlier, approaching a team of employees for their great effort is necessary. Consider the additional ideas:

- Be public. Compliment the team in a public forum, such as a team meeting or email. This helps to create a positive work environment and encourages team members to continue to perform well. I'm not fond of email compliments because in-person presentations generate sincerity.

- Be creative. Think outside the box when giving compliments. Consider giving the team a small gift or hosting a team-building event to celebrate their accomplishments.

When complimenting a work team, it's important to use positive language and focus on the team's strengths. Avoid using negative language or focusing on areas where the team could improve. This helps to create a positive work environment and encourages team members to continue to perform well.

The best practices for a leader to compliment a work team for their excellence or performance include being specific, timely, sincere, inclusive, public, creative, and consistent. By following these practices, leaders can create a positive work environment and encourage their team members to continue to perform well.

Spontaneous team compliments are a great way for leaders to show their appreciation for their team members in a more informal and personal way. Here are some ways that a leader can do spontaneous team compliments:

1. Use a whiteboard or bulletin board. Create a whiteboard or bulletin board in a common area where team members can write compliments or words of encouragement to each other. This allows team members to give compliments to each other spontaneously and in a relaxed environment.

2. Leave a note. Leave a handwritten note on a team member's desk or workstation, complimenting them on a recent accomplishment or simply thanking them for their hard work. This small gesture can make a big impact and show team members that their contributions are valued.

3. Give a shout-out in a meeting. During a team meeting, give a spontaneous compliment to a team member who has done exceptional work or gone above and beyond. This

shows that you are paying attention to their work and that you appreciate their efforts.

4. Send an email. Send a spontaneous compliment to a team member via email, thanking them for their hard work and recognizing their contributions. This can be a quick and easy way to show appreciation, especially if the team member is working remotely or in a different location.

5. Host a team-building activity. Host a team-building activity that allows team members to give spontaneous compliments to each other. For example, you can have team members write compliments on sticky notes and stick them to a board or have them take turns complimenting each other during a team-building exercise.

Spontaneous team compliments are a great way for leaders to show appreciation for their team members in a more informal and personal way. By using a whiteboard, leaving a note, giving a shout-out in a meeting, sending an email, or hosting a team-building activity, leaders can create a positive work environment and boost team morale.

As an example, the following spontaneous compliment came to an employee, Thaylor, who works in the city of Fort Collins' streets department. His crew chief, Larry Gonzales, gave Thaylor a handwritten note that said, "Thank you, Thaylor, for helping us out when we're shorthanded and for helping out with our Salt Cars. You're a joy to be around." This was written on a stationary note card with the city's logo and signed as "Gonzo," Crew Chief Gonzales' nickname. This is exactly what motivates employees and makes them feel appreciated and valued. The personal touch of the note being handwritten with a personal signature is a classy touch and a sign of an experienced leader.

Leaders who have a reputation for giving credit to others include Warren Buffett and Oprah Winfrey. Buffett is known for recognizing the contributions of his team members and often credits them for his success. Oprah Winfrey is also known for her generosity and willingness to recognize the hard work of her employees and colleagues.

Books and podcasts for leaders who know how to give credit and compliments include:

- *The Art of Possibility* by Rosamund Stone Zander and Benjamin Zander
- *The Power of Positive Leadership* by Jon Gordon
- *HBR IdeaCast* by *Harvard Business Review.*

These resources provide valuable insights into the importance of giving credit and recognition to others and offer practical advice on how to do so effectively.

I'm pretty sure that Chad Holiday got his quote from Harry Truman. Here's a quote from Harry S. Truman, the thirty-third president of the United States, about who gets the credit: "It is amazing what you can accomplish if you do not care who gets the credit."

This quote emphasizes the importance of working together as a team and focusing on the accomplishment of the task at hand, rather than personal recognition. It encourages individuals to put their egos aside and work collaboratively towards a common goal, which can lead to greater success and fulfillment for all involved.

"A true leader will always elevate and allocate credit for achievements to his/her team members, without the need to claim the spotlight for themselves," said Brian Holst, executive corporate attorney for Elevations Credit Union.

CHAPTER 16

WHAT DO YOU STAND FOR?

As a leader, it is important to know what you stand for. This means having a clear understanding of your values and principles and being willing to take a stand on important issues, even when it may be difficult or unpopular.

Unfortunately, many leaders vacillate or waffle when faced with tough decisions. They may be swayed by outside pressures or fear of criticism, and as a result, fail to take decisive action. However, the most effective leaders are those who take a stand, regardless of peer pressure, and are not afraid to stand behind their decisions.

In fact, some of the best examples of this kind of leadership can be found in very small business owners. These entrepreneurs may not have the same level of resources or influence as larger corporations, but they are often fiercely committed to their values and principles and are willing to take bold action to defend them.

To learn more about the importance of taking a stand as a leader, there are many helpful resources available. Some recommended books on this topic include:

- *Start with Why* by Simon Sinek
- *The Courage to Be Disliked* by Ichiro Kishimi and Fumitake Koga

- *Dare to Lead* by Brené Brown.

Additionally, podcasts such as *The Tim Ferriss Show* and *How I Built This* often feature interviews with successful entrepreneurs who share their insights on leadership and taking a stand.

It is crucial to know what you stand for and be willing to take a stand on important issues. By doing so, you can inspire others, build trust and credibility, and ultimately drive meaningful change.

Here are some methods and best practices a leader can utilize to take a stand:

1. Identify and clarify your values. Before you can take a stand, you need to have a clear understanding of your beliefs and values. Take time to reflect on what is most important to you and use this as a foundation for your decision-making.

2. Do your research. Before taking a stand on a particular issue, make sure you have done your due diligence. This means gathering as much information as possible, consulting with experts, and considering different perspectives. For the most part, "knee-jerk reactions" don't work.

3. Communicate clearly. Once you have taken a stand, it is important to communicate your position clearly and effectively. This means being transparent about your thought process, explaining your reasoning, and being open to feedback and questions.

4. Stay focused on your goals. Taking a stand can be challenging and may involve facing criticism or pushback. It is important to stay focused on your goals and the values that underlie your decision and to be willing to make tough choices in service of these goals.

5. Lead by example. As a leader, you can model the behaviors and values that you want to see in others. By taking a stand on issues that matter to you, you can inspire others to do the same and create a culture of courage and integrity.

6. Be willing to adapt. Finally, it is important to be open to feedback and to adapt your position as needed. Taking a stand does not mean being inflexible or unwilling to change your mind in the face of new information or evidence. Rather, it means being willing to stand up for what you believe in while remaining open to growth and learning.

Some examples of businesses and their leaders who have taken a stand on important issues are:

- Art Acevedo, who was the chief of police in Houston, Texas, and now is the interim police chief of Aurora, Colorado, sets the example of taking a stand. In 2018, after a mass shooting at a high school in Santa Fe, Texas, Chief Acevedo called for stricter gun control measures, including universal background checks and limits on high-capacity magazines. He also criticized politicians who offered "thoughts and prayers" without taking concrete action to prevent gun violence.

Chief Acevedo is a vocal advocate for police reform and implemented several changes in the Houston Police Department to improve transparency and accountability. For example, he requires officers to wear body cameras and has publicly released video footage in cases of police misconduct.

Overall, Chief Acevedo demonstrates a willingness to take a stand on important issues, even when it is politically unpopular or controversial. His leadership helped to make the Houston Police Department responsive to the needs of the community and helped inspire other law enforcement agencies to adopt similar reforms.

Langer, Andy. May 23, 2018. The National Podcast of Texas. "Houston Police Chief Art Acevedo Speaks about his Controversial Gun Rights Stance". Accessed April 24, 2023, https://www.texasmonthly.com/podcast/art-acevedo-podcast/.

- Warby Parker. Neil Blumenthal and Dave Gilboa, co-founders of Warby Parker, are vocal advocates for ethical business practices and social responsibility. The company has a "Buy a Pair, Give a Pair" program that donates eyeglasses to people in need and has also launched several initiatives to support education and other social causes.
- One example of a city manager who took a stand for the better good of the community, even when it was unpopular, is Rick Cole, the former city manager of Santa Monica, California. In 2018, he led an effort to pass a ballot measure that would increase taxes on certain types of businesses to fund investments in affordable housing and early childhood education.

The measure faced opposition from business groups, who argued that it would harm the local economy and lead to job losses. Despite these concerns, Cole stood behind the proposal, arguing that it was necessary to address the city's growing affordability crisis and to provide support for families with young children.

Ultimately, the measure was narrowly defeated, but Cole's willingness to take a stand on an issue that was important to him and to the community showed his commitment to improving the lives of Santa Monica residents. During his tenure as city manager, he also implemented several other initiatives aimed at promoting sustainability, reducing traffic congestion, and improving public safety.

- A fire chief who took a stand for the betterment of the fire department and the community is Dennis Rubin, who served as the fire chief of Washington D.C. from 2007 to 2011. During his tenure, Chief Rubin was a vocal advocate for firefighter safety and worked to improve the department's equipment and training programs. He also implemented several community outreach initiatives aimed at promoting fire prevention and educating residents about the dangers of fires.

One decision that Chief Rubin made that demonstrated his commitment to firefighter safety was to require all firefighters to always wear personal protective equipment (PPE), even when responding to routine calls. This decision was controversial at the time, as some firefighters argued that it was unnecessary and could slow down response times. However, Rubin stood behind the policy, arguing that it was necessary to protect firefighters from the risks of cancer and other occupational hazards.

Ultimately, Rubin's decision to require PPE for all firefighters was widely praised and has since become standard practice in many fire departments across the country. His leadership and commitment to firefighter safety helped to improve the culture and operations of the Washington D.C. Fire Department and set an example for other fire chiefs to follow.

Werner, Charles. June 30, 2008. "Dennis L. Rubin, DC's Fire Chief," https://www.firehouse.com/home/article/10492754/dennis-l-rubin-dcs-fire-chief.

- One last example of a mayor who was known for waffling and not taking a stance is Chicago Mayor Rahm Emanuel. During his tenure, Emanuel was often criticized for his reluctance to take bold action on controversial issues, such as police reform, education, and economic inequality.

For instance, in the aftermath of the high-profile shooting of Laquan McDonald by a Chicago police officer in 2014, Emanuel was criticized for his slow and ineffective response. Many activists and community leaders called for him to take decisive action to address issues of police brutality and systemic racism in the

Chicago Police Department, but Emanuel was seen as hesitant to take a strong stand.

Emanuel was also criticized for his handling of education issues, including the closure of dozens of public schools in predominantly black and low-income neighborhoods. Critics argued that the closures were part of a larger pattern of disinvestment in these communities and that Emanuel was not doing enough to address the root causes of educational inequality.

Overall, Emanuel's reputation as a waffling mayor who was reluctant to take a strong stand on controversial issues was a major factor in his decision not to seek reelection in 2019.

Cassella, Brian. *Chicago Tribune*. 2015. Accessed April 24, 2023, https://www.chicagotribune.com/politics/ct-met-cb-rahm-emanuel-accomplishments-controversies-20190515-story.html.

These are just a few examples of leaders who have taken a stand on important issues. There are many others who are using their businesses as a platform for positive change.

"If you don't stand for something, you will fall for everything." This adage is attributed to Alexander Hamilton, Peter Marshall, and others.

"Effective leaders are faithful behind the scenes. Character is not developed during epic moments in life that everyone sees that might lead to the fifteen minutes of fame, but in the hundreds of little decisions every day that often go unnoticed," said Mark Driscoll, retired FNBO Colorado marketing president.

CHAPTER 17

LEADING FROM WITHIN

Effective leadership begins with a deep understanding of oneself. Leaders who know themselves and their own qualities are better equipped to lead and inspire others. This chapter will explore the concept of leading from within, including how leaders can identify their own qualities and how they can use these qualities to lead both within and outside of their organization.

Self-knowledge: The key to leading from within

Before leaders can lead others, they must first lead themselves. This means having a deep understanding of their own strengths, weaknesses, and values. Self-knowledge is essential for effective leadership because it allows leaders to:

- Identify their own unique qualities and how they can use them to inspire and motivate others
- Understand their own biases and how they may impact their leadership decisions

- Develop empathy and emotional intelligence, which are essential for building strong relationships with team members and stakeholders

The most challenging assessment is self-evaluation. It entails understanding your own identity, recognizing your limitations, and identifying the resources that can support your leadership and success. This may require surrounding yourself with individuals who possess greater intelligence than yourself.

Tools and resources for self-discovery

There are several resources and tools that leaders can use to gain a better understanding of themselves, including:

1. Personality assessments such as the Myers-Briggs Type Indicator or the Enneagram
2. Leadership coaching or mentoring. There are several resources available for leaders to find leadership coaching or mentoring, including professional associations.

Many professional associations offer leadership development programs and mentorship opportunities for their members. Here are some professional associations that offer coaching and mentoring programs for leaders:

a. International Coach Federation (ICF). The ICF is a global organization dedicated to advancing the coaching profession. They offer mentor coaching programs for coaches, as well as leadership coaching programs for executives and managers.
b. Association for Talent Development (ATD). The ATD is a professional association for learning and development professionals. They offer mentorship programs for

members, as well as leadership development programs and coaching certification.

c. National Association of Corporate Directors (NACD). The NACD is a membership organization for corporate directors. They offer leadership development programs and coaching for board members and executives.

d. Society for Human Resource Management (SHRM). The SHRM is a professional association for HR professionals. They offer mentorship programs for members, as well as leadership development programs and coaching certification.

e. Institute of Coaching (IOC). The IOC is a non-profit organization dedicated to promoting coaching research and education. They offer mentoring programs for coaches, as well as coaching certification and leadership development programs.

f. International Leadership Association (ILA). The ILA is a global organization focused on advancing leadership theory and practice. They offer mentorship programs for members, as well as leadership coaching and development programs.

Remember, there are many other professional associations out there that may offer coaching and mentoring programs for leaders in specific industries or fields. It's worth doing some research to find the right association for your needs and goals as a leader. Here are more references and examples:

- Business schools often have executive coaching or mentorship programs for current and aspiring leaders.
- Networking events. Attending networking events can be a great way to meet other leaders and find potential mentors or coaches.
- Online resources. There are several online resources available for leaders, including leadership blogs, webinars,

and podcasts. These can be a great way to learn from other leaders and gain new insights into leadership.

- Leadership development programs. Many organizations offer leadership development programs that include coaching or mentoring as part of the program.
- Personal referrals. Sometimes the best way to find a mentor or coach is through personal referrals. Ask for recommendations from colleagues, friends, or family members who may know of someone who could help you. When looking for a mentor or coach, it's important to find someone who has experience and expertise in your industry or field, and who shares your values and leadership style. Remember that these mentorship and coaching relationships are personal, so it's important to find someone you feel comfortable working with and who can provide you with the support and guidance you need to achieve your leadership goals.

Journaling and self-reflection exercises can be powerful tools for leaders to gain self-awareness and improve their leadership skills. Here are some tips for effective journaling and self-reflection exercises:

a. Set aside dedicated time. Schedule a regular time for journaling and self-reflection and treat it as a non-negotiable appointment with yourself. Try to find a quiet and comfortable space where you can focus and reflect without distractions.

b. Use prompts or questions. To get started with journaling and self-reflection, consider using prompts or questions to guide your reflection. For example, you might reflect on a recent leadership challenge you faced or consider your personal values and how they align with your leadership style.

   c. Write freely. When journaling, it's important to write freely and without judgment. Don't worry about grammar or spelling, and don't censor yourself. Simply write down your thoughts and feelings as they come up.

   d. Reflect on your experiences. Self-reflection exercises can be an opportunity to reflect on your experiences as a leader. Consider what you learned from a recent success or failure or reflect on the feedback you've received from team members or stakeholders.

   e. Evaluate your progress. Regular self-reflection can help you track your progress as a leader. Consider setting goals for yourself and tracking your progress over time through your journal.

Journaling and self-reflection exercises are personal and should be tailored to your own needs and preferences as a leader. Whether you prefer free writing or guided prompts, the most important thing is to set aside dedicated time for reflection and to approach it with an open and curious mindset. By doing so, you can gain valuable insights into your own strengths and weaknesses as a leader and make meaningful improvements to your leadership style over time.

Feedback from team members and stakeholders is another way to gain self-awareness. The best way to accept feedback from team members and stakeholders is to approach it with an open and receptive mindset. Here are some tips for accepting feedback effectively:

   a. Listen actively. When someone is giving you feedback, give them your full attention. Listen carefully to what they are saying, and ask clarifying questions if you need more information.

   b. Avoid becoming defensive. It can be tempting to become defensive when receiving feedback, especially if it is critical. However, this can shut down communication and prevent you from learning from the feedback. Instead, try to remain open and curious.

c.   Thank the person for their feedback. It takes courage to give feedback, so it's important to acknowledge and thank the person for taking the time to share their thoughts with you.

d.   Reflect on the feedback. After receiving feedback, take some time to reflect on what was said. Consider the validity of the feedback, and how you can use it to improve your performance.

e.   Take action. If the feedback is valid, take action to address any issues or concerns that were raised. This demonstrates to your team members and stakeholders that you take their feedback seriously and are committed to improving.

Ultimately, accepting feedback is an important part of being an effective leader. By approaching it with an open and curious mindset, you can learn from your team members and stakeholders and use their feedback to improve your performance and build stronger relationships with those around you.

Leading from within the organization

Once leaders have a strong understanding of themselves, they can use their qualities to lead within their organization. This means:

- Developing a clear vision and mission for the organization
- Communicating effectively with team members and stakeholders
- Building strong relationships based on trust and respect
- Empowering team members to take ownership of their work and make meaningful contributions to the organization

Leading outside the organization

Leaders also have a responsibility to represent their organization outside of the workplace. This means:

- Demonstrating strong ethical and moral values
- Building strong relationships with stakeholders, including customers, partners, and community members
- Being a thought leader in their industry and sharing their knowledge and expertise with other
- Developing a strong personal brand that aligns with the values and mission of their organization

The psychology of leadership: Are leaders born or made?

While some people may have natural leadership qualities, effective leadership is a skill that can be learned and developed over time. The psychological profile of a good leader includes qualities such as:

- Emotional intelligence
- Resilience
- Empathy
- Creativity
- Visionary thinking

Examples of non-leaders who lead from within

Leadership is not limited to those with formal leadership titles. There are many examples of non-leaders who lead from within, including:

- Team members who take initiative and go above and beyond in their work

- Community members who organize and lead grassroots initiatives
- Thought leaders who share their knowledge and expertise to inspire others

Tools and resources for leading from within

There are several books, podcasts, and other resources that can help leaders develop their skills and lead from within, including:

- *The Power of Vulnerability* by Brené Brown
- *Dare to Lead* by Brené Brown
- *Leaders Eat Last* by Simon Sinek
- *The Art of Possibility* by Rosamund Stone Zander and Benjamin Zander
- *The Tim Ferriss Show* podcast

Conclusion

Leading from within is essential for effective leadership. Leaders who know their own strengths, weaknesses, and values are better equipped to lead their organization and represent it outside of the workplace. By using tools and resources to develop their skills and qualities, leaders can inspire and motivate their team members and stakeholders to achieve their full potential.

"Leadership is not about being in charge. It's about taking care of those in your charge," said Simon Sinek. This quote emphasizes the idea that leadership is not just about titles or authority, but about taking responsibility for the well-being and success of those you lead.

To lead from within, you must have a deep understanding of yourself and your own qualities and use those qualities to inspire and motivate those around you. Ultimately, the best leaders are those who put the needs of their team members and stakeholders first, and who are committed to creating a positive and productive work environment for everyone involved.

"I learned a long time ago that God is first. If you have from within such as tenacity, dedication, persistence, and commitment anything is possible. My parents taught me well!" said Dr. Lupe Salazar, an educator, instructor, writer, inspirational speaker, and consultant.

Dr. Salazar is undoubtedly deserving of the Oliver P. Pennock Distinguished Service Award that she received. Lupe's life is a shining example of a labor of love for education and people, and she personifies this in her everyday actions. Her contributions to Colorado State University and the community are clear through her selfless dedication to helping others. Dr. Salazar consistently goes above and beyond expectations to promote human interests, and her intuition and experience have helped many students take the right steps toward success, particularly through El Centro at Colorado State.

Dr. Salazar's exceptional work and passion were also highlighted in a historical documentary film on Hispanic Leadership produced by the city of Fort Collins. Listening to her interview alone is enough to realize her unwavering commitment and determination (https://youtu.be/yzuqlFI4cXA).

"A crucial aspect of leadership is how we deal with perceived failures. The actual 'failure' is often overshadowed by how poorly it is dealt with after the fact. Leaders who are afraid of failing pass that sentiment on to their teams, constricting and inhibiting creativity, initiative, and innovation. I would ask that leaders take a hard look at their beliefs around failure and remain open to moving past the failure to the learning phase. If we don't learn from our mistakes, we will certainly repeat them," said Kate Brown, founder of Boulder Organic Foods, which is sold nationwide.

Harry Safstrom, the CEO of Confluential Consulting, wrote a LinkedIn post on July 21, 2015, in which he praised Kate Brown as a genuine, thoughtful, and forward-thinking leader who understands the importance of fostering an inclusive and energized company culture. Safstrom also commended Brown for her hands-on approach to leadership, her commitment to continuous learning, and her deep understanding of her business at all levels.

In May 2015, *O: The Oprah Magazine* featured a story about Kate Brown's success as the founder of Boulder Organic Foods. The article, which can be found at https://www.oprah.com/food/boulder-organic-foods-how-to-start-food-business, highlights Brown's entrepreneurial spirit and her dedication to creating high-quality, organic food products.

CNBC also wrote about Kate Brown's achievements in an article published on September 2, 2016. The article, available at https://www.cnbc.com/2016/09/02/organic-food-doesnt-have-to-clean-out-your-walleat.html, explores Brown's efforts to make organic food more accessible and affordable to consumers, while still maintaining the integrity and sustainability of her business. Kate is currently on the board of directors for Elevations Credit Union, Boulder, Colorado.

CHAPTER 18

EFFECTIVE MEETINGS THROUGH LEADERSHIP

Effective meetings are essential for any organization to achieve its goals and objectives. A productive meeting is one that results in clear communication, collaboration, and decision-making among the participants. In today's fast-paced and dynamic environment, meetings are a necessary tool to ensure that everyone is on the same page and working towards the same goals. Therefore, it is crucial to plan and conduct meetings effectively to ensure that they are productive and achieve their intended purpose. This chapter will provide insights into the best practices for conducting meetings that will help organizations improve their overall performance.

In 1999, when I first became the mayor of Fort Collins, our weekly Monday leadership meetings with the city manager and department heads were an unproductive, three-hour-long marathon. We would set agendas and review department issues, but progress was slow, and discussions often veered off-topic. After my first meeting, I decided to shake things up by announcing that all future meetings would be no more than one hour. Initially, there were skeptical faces and disbelief that such a change was possible.

However, after receiving private emails from colleagues expressing their support and their willingness to be part of the solution, I knew we were on the right track. The following week, our meeting lasted less than an hour, including a catered lunch, and we accomplished everything we did the previous week. For the next six years, we continued to have productive, solution-oriented meetings that never exceeded sixty minutes. This change helped us to stay focused and achieve our goals efficiently, proving that effective meetings don't need to be long and unproductive. We always had an agenda that was very specific, attainable, and measurable (SAM).

I am not naive about the fact that some meetings require more time. These often take the form of scheduled committee or board "work sessions" or retreats, which involve a pre-planned agenda that includes breaks and breakout sessions. In these meetings, everyone knows what to expect.

When preparing agendas for any meeting, it's important to set time limits for each agenda item, specifying the purpose, agenda, allotted time, and the person presenting. This will help ensure that the meeting stays on track and that all important items are addressed within the allotted time.

Since my term as mayor ended in 2005, I have conducted classes for various groups on how to hold effective meetings. During my term, I was appointed as a board director for another organization and offered my services for free to help shorten their lengthy meetings, which typically lasted three hours. After meeting with the chair and vice chair for a couple of sessions, they became convinced that substantial reductions were achievable. I commend them for their boldness in taking action to restructure the meetings, resulting in a remarkable 50 percent reduction in the required time. I truly admire their leadership and courage in "grabbing the bull by the horns."

I vividly remember a time when I was having dinner with friends at the Three Margaritas restaurant in Fort Collins. As we were enjoying our meal, a little boy, who looked about seven years old, approached our table and asked me if I was the mayor. I confirmed that I was, and he blurted out that his dad said, "You can have that job!" I couldn't help but chuckle at his innocence and handed him my business card. His father looked with eyes wide open and placed his hand on his forehead and shook his head. It was a great experience, and we just waved at each other.

As I reflected on that incident, I realized that the little boy's father understood something crucial about being a mayor—the importance of clear and concise communication. As the mayor, regular communication with people at all levels of the organization, and the public are complex and essential. However, I've always believed that simplicity equals transparency, and I've developed that simple formula to ensure effective communication, especially during public meetings.

By being clear and concise in my communication, I can run functional meetings that are productive and efficient. No more beating around the bush or lengthy discussions that go nowhere. Instead, I've learned to get straight to the point, and it has made all the difference in my one-on-one meetings, boards, and group meetings. So thank you to that little boy and his father for reminding me of the importance of simplicity in communication.

Here are some key ways of running an effective meeting, along with best practices and resources:

1. Set clear goals and objectives. Before the meeting, it's important to set clear goals and objectives. This will help to keep the meeting focused and ensure that everyone is on the same page. One effective way to do this is to create an agenda that outlines the key topics and goals for the meeting.

2. Invite relevant participants. Invite only the germane participants who can contribute to the discussion and decision-making process. This will help keep the meeting focused and ensure that everyone has a chance to participate.

3. Use technology to enhance collaboration. Technology can be a great tool for enhancing collaboration and engagement during meetings. Tools such as video conferencing, virtual whiteboards, and collaborative document editing can help keep participants engaged and focused.

4. Encourage participation. Encourage all participants to contribute to the discussion and decision-making process. One effective way to do this is to use techniques such as round-robin or brainstorming to ensure that everyone has a chance to share their ideas.

5. Keep the meeting on track. One of the key challenges of running an effective meeting is keeping it on track. To do this, it's important to establish ground rules at the beginning of the meeting and impose them throughout. This can include guidelines for speaking time, staying on topic, and avoiding distractions.

6. Follow up after the meeting. Follow up after the meeting with a summary of the key decisions and action items. This will help to ensure that everyone is on the same page and that progress is being made.

I always like to say, take your PAL with you: the purpose of the meeting, the agenda for the meeting, and the length of the meeting. In the origination of the PAL concept, the acronym has no significance.

The PAL method of having meetings is a framework developed by Patrick Lencioni, author of the book *Death by Meeting: A Leadership Fable...About Solving the Most Painful Problem in Business.* The framework is designed to help leaders run more effective meetings by providing a structure for different types of meetings.

PAL stands for:

1. Daily check-in. The daily check-in is a brief meeting that takes place at the beginning of each day. The purpose of this meeting is to align team members around their

Ray Martinez

priorities for the day, identify potential obstacles, and ensure that everyone is on the same page.

2. Weekly tactical. The weekly tactical is a longer meeting that takes place once a week. The purpose of this meeting is to review progress on projects, discuss priorities for the coming week, and identify any issues or roadblocks that need to be addressed.

3. Monthly strategic. The monthly strategic is a longer meeting that takes place once a month. The purpose of this meeting is to review progress on strategic initiatives, discuss long-term goals, and make decisions about major initiatives or investments.

The PAL method is designed to ensure that meetings are focused and productive, and that team members are aligned around key priorities and goals. By establishing clear objectives for each type of meeting, leaders can ensure that meetings are not only effective but also efficient and engaging for all participants.

Implementing the PAL method can help leaders to streamline their meetings and reduce the amount of time spent in unproductive meetings, ultimately improving organizational performance, and driving success.

As an observer of city council meetings and as the mayor, I've seen firsthand how important it is for the mayor to keep the meeting moving in sequential order, helping council members frame their statements with brevity, and managing the citizen public forums with order and sensibility.

When meetings go awry, it can be difficult to keep the council focused on the agenda without straying off into other topics. This is where Robert's Rules of Order come in. By following these established rules, the council can stay focused on the agenda, avoid unnecessary delays and distractions, and ensure that all members have an equal opportunity to participate and contribute to the discussion.

It is crucial for the mayor to understand and implement these rules in a fair and consistent manner to keep the council meetings productive and effective. However, it doesn't mean overregulating a meeting that becomes too cumbersome for people to follow or that creates an atmosphere of apathy.

One example of a mayor allowing a meeting to get out of hand was in the city of Ferguson, Missouri, in 2014. The city council meetings were held in a small room that could only accommodate a limited number of people, leading to tensions and frustrations among citizens who were unable to attend. When the meetings did take place, the mayor, James Knowles III, was criticized for his handling of the public comments section. Citizens were given only three minutes each to speak, and Mayor Knowles was accused of cutting off speakers mid-sentence and ignoring comments that were critical of the city's police department.

As the city became the focus of national attention following the shooting of Michael Brown, tensions at the city council meetings continued to escalate. At one meeting, protesters disrupted the proceedings, chanting and shouting over the mayor and council members. Mayor Knowles was criticized for not doing enough to maintain order and failing to address the concerns of the citizens.

Overall, the situation in Ferguson highlighted the importance of effective leadership in managing city council meetings. When the mayor fails to keep the meeting moving in chronological order, help council members frame their statements with brevity, and manage citizen public forums with order and sensibility, it can lead to tensions and frustrations among citizens and detract from the value of the council.

In our society, dialogue is more important than debate because dialogue seeks to find solutions to problems, while debate is often focused on highlighting differences and winning arguments. Dialogue is a process of conversation where people share their ideas, perspectives, and experiences with the goal of understanding and finding common ground. It is a way to foster communication and build relationships, even among people with different viewpoints.

On the other hand, a debate is more focused on proving one's point and winning the argument, often at the expense of relationships and collaboration.

When we engage in dialogue, we open ourselves up to new perspectives and ideas, which can lead to creative solutions and a deeper understanding of the issues at hand. In contrast, debate can create an adversarial environment, where people are less likely to listen to one another and more focused on winning the argument.

Meetings should be out of necessity. The last thing anyone wants is "more bloody meetings." The three laws of meetings are to unite, focus, and mobilize the group. When uniting the group, there can be some frustration or aggression when there is strong opposition to the type of anticipated discussion. Give them a chance to let off some steam and don't take sides. Bring in the others and stick to the facts.

Next, keep the group focused so they don't get off point and stay alert. I like to say, "Keep a hand on the wheel, and don't hesitate to paraphrase what someone has said for clarity."

Finally, activate the group by swiftly circling the room to identify any missing elements in the discussion. Make sure to document suggestions and expand upon the ideas presented.

When reaching a consensus about a decision, state the purpose and alternatives for a consensus discussion and determine if you have a "yes vote" or agreement. Then you can move on to the next topic.

Bullet guidelines for effective consensus

- Involve everyone in the discussion.
- Explore the alternatives.
- Listen to what the other person is saying.
- Identify actual problems, not symptoms.
- Be careful of quick solutions.
- Encourage differences to clarify issues.

- Avoid conflict-reducing techniques, such as majority vote, averaging, coin flips, etc.
- Yield only to positions that have objective and sound foundations.
- Try not to compete.
- Allocate your time carefully.
- Always strive for the best answer.
- Data makes consensus easier.

The three conditions for consensus are:

1. I believe that you understand my point of view.
2. I believe that I understand your point of view.
3. Whether or not I prefer this decision, I will support it because it was arrived at in an open and fair manner.

If you want to read more about this, James Madden of London, Ontario, published his ideas in *A Practical Guide on Consensus-Base Decision Making*: https://www.tamarackcommunity.ca/hubfs/Resources/Tools/Practical%20Guide%20for%20Consensus-Based%20Decision%20Making.pdf.

Here is another method of having meetings utilizing an older tool that still works today:

The plan-do-check-act (PDCA) cycle is a management method used to continuously improve processes and achieve organizational goals. It involves four stages: plan, do, check, and act.

In the planning stage, goals and objectives are set, and plans are developed to achieve them. In the do stage, the plans are put into action. The check stage involves monitoring and evaluating the results of the actions taken in the do stage. Finally, in the acting stage, any necessary changes are made to improve the process, and the cycle starts again.

The PDCA cycle is a useful tool for organizations to improve their processes, reduce waste, and enhance customer satisfaction.

What I like about the PDCA is that it is simple and corresponds to the way human beings operate. It also provides us with a common language and a clear model that we can use to improve quality.

Resources to reflect on:

1. *Dialogue: The Art of Thinking Together* by William Isaacs. This book provides a comprehensive guide to the art of dialogue, including practical techniques for fostering productive conversations.
2. *Crucial Conversations: Tools for Talking When Stakes Are High* by Kerry Patterson, Joseph Grenny, Ron McMillan, and Al Switzler. This book provides practical tools for having difficult conversations, including strategies for fostering dialogue and building relationships.
3. "The Difference Between Dialogue and Debate." This article from the *Harvard Business Review* provides a clear explanation of the differences between dialogue and debate, and why dialogue is more important for effective communication and collaboration.
4. "Dialogue vs. Debate: Which One Is More Important?" This article from *Psychology Today* explores the benefits of dialogue over debate, and how it can lead to more effective problem-solving and collaboration. There are numerous articles on the Internet about dialogue versus debate.
5. The Harvard Business Review has a great article titled "Leadership is a Conversation" by Boris Graysberg and Michael Slind, from the magazine 2012.

https://hbr.org/2012/06/leadership-is-a-conversation

In summary, dialogue is more important than debate because it fosters communication, builds relationships, and seeks to find solutions to problems. Engaging in dialogue can lead to more effective problem-solving, deeper understanding, and stronger relationships, making it an essential tool for effective leadership and collaboration.

Other resources for running meetings:

- *The Effective Executive: The Definitive Guide to Getting the Right Things Done* by Peter F. Drucker. This book provides a comprehensive guide to effective leadership, including best practices for running effective meetings.
- *Death by Meeting: A Leadership Fable . . . About Solving the Most Painful Problem in Business* by Patrick Lencioni. This book provides a fictional account of a company struggling with ineffective meetings and provides practical strategies for improving meeting effectiveness.
- *The 7 Habits of Highly Effective People: Powerful Lessons in Personal Change* by Stephen R. Covey. This book provides a comprehensive guide to personal and professional effectiveness, including best practices for running effective meetings.
- "The Harvard Business Review Guide to Making Every Meeting Matter." This guide provides practical tips and best practices for running effective meetings, including strategies for setting clear goals, encouraging participation, and following up after the meeting.
- MeetingSift. This online tool provides a range of features to help run more effective meetings, including real-time collaboration, interactive presentations, and data-driven decision-making.

The six general types or most common types of meetings:

1. Status update meetings
2. Information sharing meetings
3. Decision-making meetings

4. Problem-solving meetings
5. Innovation meetings
6. Team-building meetings

Dave Carlson is the council commissioner and trustee of the Greater Colorado Council, Boy Scouts of America, making him the highest-ranking executive officer in the council who wears the scouting uniform. As a member of the Key Six, he works with other volunteers and professional staff to lead the council, which includes the chairman, president, treasurer, president-elect, and scout executive (CEO). Regarding organizational meetings, Dave provided the following remarks:

> It has been said that the only industries that profit from most organizational meetings are those that make coffee and bagels. Throughout my business career, I have experienced countless hours of wasted productivity and thought due to poorly organized and led meetings.
>
> In volunteer and non-profit organizations like the BSA, poorly organized and led meetings can result in wasted time and delay decision-making and action. To combat this issue, a good leader should only hold necessary meetings with a specific agenda and set start and end times, assigned participants, and focus on staying on topic. Additionally, a thoughtful leader should conduct meetings with respect and consideration for all participants, clearly stated objectives and schedules, and a goal of accomplishing the meeting's mission. If a leader cannot clearly articulate the purpose and mission of a meeting, they should not hold it. It's important to know when to end an unproductive meeting.

Unfortunately, many meetings are held for the wrong reasons and can delay decision-making and action. Some meetings are held under the guise of "collaboration" or to encourage team participation but are poorly formulated and cause more team dissent than consent. As such, it's essential to have well-organized and purposeful meetings to ensure productivity and positive outcomes.

Holding stand-up meetings can be an effective way to increase productivity in the workplace. According to a study conducted by *Harvard Business Review*, stand-up meetings can reduce the length of meetings by up to 34 percent and increase engagement among team members. By standing, team members tend to stay more focused and alert, which can lead to more efficient and effective communication.

Additionally, stand-up meetings help promote a sense of urgency and accountability among team members, as they are more likely to stay on task and avoid lengthy tangents. Overall, incorporating stand-up meetings into a company's culture leads to improved productivity and improved communication among team members. (Source: Harvard Business Review, "The Science of Meetings," by Steven G. Rogelberg). Rogelberg also writes a book called *The Surprising Science of Meetings: How You Can Lead Your Team to Peak Performance.*

This is a great article to read for more details about conducting standup meetings. https://martinfowler.com/articles/itsNotJustStandingUp.html#WeStandUpToKeepTheMeetingShort.

While staying at the Omni Hotel in Broomfield, Colorado, for a business meeting, I witnessed a remarkable scene in the morning. A group of hotel employees gathered in the main lobby, off to the side, for a standup meeting to kickstart their day. As I was seated nearby, I had the opportunity to overhear their discussion, which left a strong impression on me. The team leader began by expressing compliments from the previous day and providing words of encouragement for the day ahead. They proceeded to address necessary improvements, identifying individuals responsible for leading those efforts. Finally, they opened the floor for comments, ensuring active participation from everyone present. Remarkably, the entire meeting concluded within fifteen minutes.

From my perspective as an outsider, the meeting appeared highly productive, fostering a positive and encouraging atmosphere. It was evident that each person left with a clear understanding of their objectives for the day. Even as a spectator, I felt well-informed about the tasks at hand.

In summary, running an effective meeting requires clear goals, relevant participants, technology-enhanced collaboration, encouraged participation, staying on track, and follow-up after the meeting. Utilizing best practices and resources such as books and tools can help leaders to improve their meeting effectiveness and drive organizational success.

"Meetings are a waste of time if they are not conducted efficiently, but the right meeting at the right time can move mountains," said Richard Branson, founder of Virgin Group.

CHAPTER 19

PREDICTIVE LEADERSHIP

Leadership is an essential element of any organization, and it is the process of influencing people to achieve a common goal. A good leader must be able to anticipate future challenges and trends and make decisions that will help the organization stay ahead of the curve. Predictive leadership is a new concept that has emerged in recent years, and it is defined as the ability to use data and analytics to predict future trends and make informed decisions. In this chapter, we will define predictive leadership, discuss how to identify it, and explore the value of predictive leadership in organizations. In any circle that I walk in, people want predictability.

Defining predictive leadership

Predictive leadership is a leadership style that involves using data and analytics to predict future trends and make informed decisions. This type of leadership relies heavily on data analysis and predictive modeling to anticipate future challenges and opportunities. Predictive leaders are proactive in their approach and are always looking for ways to improve the organization's performance.

Identifying predictive leadership

Predictive leaders are easy to identify because they are always looking for ways to improve the organization's performance. They are proactive in their approach and are always looking for new data sources to help them make informed decisions. Predictive leaders are also very data-driven and rely heavily on analytics to make decisions. They are not afraid to take risks and are willing to experiment with new ideas and technologies.

The value of predictive leadership

Predictive leadership has several benefits for organizations. First, it allows leaders to anticipate future challenges and opportunities, which helps them make informed decisions. Predictive leaders are also better equipped to identify trends and patterns in data, which allows them to make more accurate predictions about the future. This, in turn, can help organizations stay ahead of the curve and remain competitive in their industry.

Second, predictive leadership also helps organizations become more efficient. Predictive leaders are always looking for ways to improve processes and eliminate waste. By using data and analytics, they can identify areas where the organization can be more efficient and make changes accordingly. This can help organizations save time and money, and improve overall performance.

Predictive leadership is a new and emerging concept that has the potential to revolutionize the way organizations operate. By using data and analytics to predict future trends and make informed decisions, predictive leaders can help organizations stay ahead of the curve and remain competitive in their industry. They are easy to identify because of their proactive approach and data-driven decision-making, and they bring significant value to organizations by anticipating future challenges, improving efficiency, and driving overall performance.

The psychological profile of a predictive leader can vary, but there are some common traits that are often associated with this type of leader. Here are some of the key psychological characteristics of a predictive leader:

1. Analytical thinking. Predictive leaders are known for their analytical thinking and problem-solving skills. They can analyze complex data sets and identify patterns and trends that others may not see.
2. Creativity. While predictive leaders rely heavily on data and analytics, they are also creative thinkers who are willing to experiment with new ideas and technologies.
3. Risk-taking. Predictive leaders are not afraid to take risks and are willing to try new things. They understand that innovation requires some level of risk, and they are always looking for ways to improve the organization's performance.
4. Visionary. Predictive leaders are often visionary thinkers who can see the big picture and anticipate future trends. They can develop long-term strategies that align with the organization's goals and objectives.
5. Resilience. Predictive leaders must be resilient because they are often pushing the boundaries and trying new things. They must be able to handle setbacks and failures and learn from them.
6. Emotional intelligence. Predictive leaders have strong emotional intelligence and can understand and empathize with those around them. They are effective communicators and are able to build strong relationships with their teams.
7. Continuous learning. Predictive leaders are always learning and growing. They are constantly seeking new information and knowledge to improve their decision-making and leadership skills.

Some people confuse predictive leadership with strategic planning, which is different. Strategic planning focuses on setting long-term goals, formulating a clear vision for the organization, and creating a roadmap to achieve those objectives. It involves careful analysis of the internal and external factors impacting the business, identifying strengths, weaknesses, opportunities, and threats, and developing strategies to capitalize on opportunities and mitigate risks.

While predictive leadership emphasizes adaptability and responsiveness, strategic planning provides a structured framework for aligning organizational resources and actions toward a defined vision. Both approaches are valuable in their own right, and the choice between them depends on the specific context and goals of the organization.

In summary, a predictive leader is a complex individual with a unique set of psychological traits. They are analytical, creative, risk-taking, visionary, resilient, emotionally intelligent, and always learning. These traits enable them to anticipate future trends and make informed decisions that help their organizations stay ahead of the curve.

Here are some other known leaders who are considered predictive leaders:

1. Tim Cook, CEO of Apple
2. Sundar Pichai, CEO of Google and Alphabet
3. Ginni Rometty, former CEO of IBM
4. Jack Ma, founder and former executive chairman of Alibaba Group
5. Mary Barra, CEO of General Motors
6. Reed Hastings, cofounder and CEO of Netflix
7. Satya Nadella, CEO of Microsoft
8. Jamie Dimon, CEO of JPMorgan Chase
9. Bob Iger, former CEO of Disney

These leaders have demonstrated a strong ability to anticipate and prepare for future trends and challenges in their respective industries. They have a track record of making strategic decisions that position their organizations for growth and success. Their vision, foresight, and ability to inspire and lead their teams have earned them a reputation as some of the most innovative and influential leaders of our time.

General Stanley McChrystal is a known military predictive leader. He is a retired US Army general who served as the commander of the Joint Special Operations Command (JSOC) from 2003 to 2008 and as the commander of US and NATO forces in Afghanistan from 2009 to 2010.

McChrystal is known for his ability to anticipate and prepare for future trends and challenges in military operations. He implemented a number of innovative and unconventional strategies during his time in command, including the use of small, highly trained teams to carry out targeted missions against high-value targets.

McChrystal also emphasized the importance of building strong relationships with local communities and leaders to gain their support and cooperation. His leadership style was characterized by a willingness to challenge conventional thinking and take calculated risks in pursuit of his objectives. "He was reportedly known for saying what other military leaders were thinking but were afraid to say; this was one of the reasons cited for his appointment to lead all forces in Afghanistan."

McChrystal, Stanley. *Wikipedia*. Accessed May 3, 2023, https://en.m.wikipedia.org/wiki/Stanley_A._McChrystal.

Some recommended resources:

1. *Predictive Leadership: How to Use Analytics to Drive Your Most Important Decisions* by Eric Siegel. This book provides a comprehensive guide to predictive leadership and how leaders can use analytics to make informed decisions.

2. *The Predictive Leader: How to Thrive as a Leader in the Age of Data Analytics* by Cyrille Vincey. This book explores how

leaders can use data analytics to predict future trends and make informed decisions.

3. *Predictive Analytics: The Power to Predict Who Will Click, Buy, Lie, or Die* by Eric Siegel. While not specifically about leadership, this book provides a thorough introduction to predictive analytics and how it can be used to make predictions in a variety of fields.

4. "Predictive Leadership: A New Tool for a New Age" by David Peterson. This article explores the concept of predictive leadership and how to apply predictability to make better decisions and improve organizational performance.

5. "The Predictive Leader: How to Use Artificial Intelligence to Optimize Your Leadership Style." This article from *Forbes* explores how leaders can use artificial intelligence to become more predictive and make better decisions.

6. *Predictive Analytics in HR: Connecting Data to Business Outcomes* by Tracey Smith. This book explores how predictive analytics can be used in HR to make better hiring and management decisions.

7. "The Predictive Index: A Blueprint for Leading with Data." This article from *Harvard Business Review* explores the use of predictive analytics in talent management and leadership development.

These resources provide a great starting point for anyone interested in learning more about predictive leadership and how it can be used to drive organizational success.

EPILOGUE

THE ART OF LEADING BY GETTING OUT OF YOUR OWN WAY

Jennifer Carpenter, the business development lead at Elevations Credit Union, served as a great inspiration for me to address the concept of "getting out of one's own way." This statement holds significant truth as we often find ourselves entangled in the notion that only *I* am capable of accomplishing certain tasks or goals.

As a leader, it can be easy to fall into the trap of thinking that success depends solely on your own abilities and decisions—that's where the "bottleneck" of an organization starts. However, the most effective leaders are those who understand the importance of getting out of their own way and empowering their team to achieve greatness. I think the best practices for leading by getting out of your own way are:

1. Trust your team. One of the biggest obstacles to effective leadership is the belief that you must have all the answers. However, the truth is that the best leaders are those who surround themselves with talented individuals and trust them to do their jobs. By empowering your team and giving them the autonomy to make decisions, you can create a culture of innovation and collaboration that will drive success.

2. Focus on the big picture. It's easy to get bogged down in the day-to-day operations of your organization, but the most effective leaders are those who see the bigger picture. By taking a step back and looking at the larger goals and objectives of your organization, you can help your team stay focused on what really matters. I can't express this enough: Zoom out, zoom out, zoom out.

3. Embrace failure. No one likes to fail, but the truth is that failure is an essential part of the learning process. As a leader, it's important to create a culture where failure is not only accepted but embraced as an opportunity for growth and improvement. By giving your team the freedom to experiment and try new things, you can foster a culture of innovation and creativity.

4. Communicate effectively. Effective communication is essential to successful leadership. By being transparent and open with your team, you can build trust and create a culture of teamwork. Additionally, it's important to listen to feedback from your team and be willing to make changes based on their input.

5. Lead by example. Finally, the most effective leaders are those who lead by example. By setting a positive tone and demonstrating the behavior you expect from the team, you create a culture of respect and accountability. Remember, the team is watching your every move, so it's important to model the behavior you want to see.

Leading by getting out of your own way requires a combination of trust, focus, innovation, communication, and modeling. By implementing these best practices, you can empower the team to achieve greatness and drive success for the organization.

I've come to realize that the most effective way to lead is often to step aside and let others take the lead. It means putting aside our own desires for recognition or control and instead trusting in the skills and abilities of those around us. When we do this, true growth and success can occur.

A good leader, whether leading a small group or a large organization, can make a significant impact on the quality of life for those around them. Some of our greatest leaders have never been elected or appointed to a position, yet their life-changing contributions have positively affected the lives of millions of people. Examples of such leaders include:

- Mahatma Gandhi was an Indian independence activist who led India to independence and inspired movements for civil rights and freedom across the world. "Be the change that you wish to see in the world," Gandhi said.
- Martin Luther King Jr. was an American Baptist minister and activist who led the civil rights movement in the United States from the mid-1950s until his assassination in 1968. "A genuine leader is not a searcher for consensus but a molder of consensus," King said.
- Mother Teresa was a Catholic nun who devoted her life to serving the poor and sick in India and around the world. "Do not go where the path may lead. Go instead where there is no path and leave a trail," she said. And that is exactly what she did.
- Desmond Tutu is a South African Anglican cleric and theologian who played a key role in the fight against apartheid in South Africa and received the Nobel Peace Prize in 1984. "A leader is not a dictator; leaders lead by empowering the people around them," he said.
- Cesar Chavez was an American labor leader and civil rights activist who co-founded the United Farm Workers (UFW) and fought for the rights of migrant farm workers in the United States. He was known for saying, "The fight is never about grapes or lettuce. It's always about people."

"Sometimes good leadership is getting out of your own way," said Jennifer Shepherd, in charge of mortgage sales business development for Elevations Credit Union in Fort Collins, Colorado.

Other books by Ray Martinez:

A Matter of Survival, Your Fight Against Burglars, about how to protect yourself from burglaries and personal attacks
ISBN 0-9644652-0-5

Saturday's Opinion, a collection of short stories ranging from national, state, and local issues
ISBN 0-9644652-2-1

Baby Boy-R is a memoir about Ray Martinez finding his biological mother only to discover she was a victim and thought he had died—yet finding other siblings he never knew
ISBN 978-0-595-44746-6

Growing Daily, a daily guide for daily living and learning what God teaches us each day
ISBN 9781414115436

Just Another Opinion, a collection of short stories on issues ranging from national to local issues and a second sequel to *Saturday's Opinion*
ISBN 978-0-9644652-8-2

From Darkness to Light: The Mai Tran Journey of Passion, a true story of a fifteen-year-old boy's escape from Vietnam as one of the boat people in the seventies
ISBN 978-0-9644652-6-8

The Truth About Marijuana: America's Snake Oil. Today, we are faced with the twenty-first century "snake oil" that proponents want you to believe that marijuana cures everything. Snake oil never lives up to the sellers' hype.
ISBN 978-1-4771-0532-0

Jesus Said, a book that captures some of the key biblical verses and expounds on my personal thoughts and experiences
ISBN 978-145357788-2

101 Seeds: Planting and Germinating Greatness. This publication contains heartfelt moments of reflection that inspired me over the years. It is a daily devotion for guidance and peace of mind.
ISBN: 978-1-68314-487-8

The Teachings of Jesus: a book that focuses on what Jesus taught about specifically that covers many topical examples.
ISBN: 9781669874133

Additional books are listed at www.raymartinez.com or https://rayforcouncil.com/consulting/books/

Books that Ray Martinez has been included in

The Death Merchant by Joseph C. Goulden
ISBN 0-671-49341-8

Manhunt, The Incredible Pursuit of CIA Agent Turned Terrorist by
Peter Maas
ISBN 0-394-55293-8

101 Memorable Men of Northern Colorado by Arlene Ahlbrandt
ISBN 0-9663932-8-7

Modern visions along the Poudre Valley by Phil Walker
ISBN 1-887982-13-2

Hit From Behind...Out of Perfect Timing Came Perfect Chaos... by
Jim Heckel
ISBN 978-1-60791-034-3

50 Interviews—Dream It, Live It, Love It by Don McGrath
ISBN 978-0-98229-071-2

The Blueprint: How the Democrats Won Colorado by Adam
Schrager and Rob Witwer
ISBN 978-1-936218-00-4

You can learn more about Ray Martinez at www.raymartinez.
com or by email at raymartinez31@gmail.com, Telephone:
970.690.3686

INDEX

G

H

I

Printed in the United States
by Baker & Taylor Publisher Services